"Deep and relatable. Spending forty days in Scripture along with *A Habit Called Faith* could be one of the best things you do this year. Jen is one of the greatest writers of our generation!"

Jennie Allen, *New York Times* bestselling author of *Get Out of Your Head*, founder and visionary of IF:Gathering

"No matter your faith journey, you are welcome here within these pages. Jen warmly invites readers into a forty-day experience that will forever change the root of the readers' faith. Allow yourself to become vulnerable as you take a deep dive into discovering the joy waiting on the other side of an authentic relationship with the Father."

Rebekah Lyons, bestselling author of *Rhythms of Renewal* and *You Are Free*

"As a pastor, I'm often asked for resources that aid in daily Bible reading, and I often don't know how to respond. Many Bible study resources tend to be either saccharine and superficial or turgid and inaccessible. And this is why *A Habit Called Faith* is such a needed and vital book. Jen Pollock Michel has given us a resource that has paired smart, theologically rich insight with writing that is warm and evocative. This book invites us into the story of Scripture and the stories of regular men and women who have taken up this habit of faith. And, wonderfully, Michel makes room for readers wherever they are in their life of faith—wary skeptics and longtime disciples are both welcomed in and helped by this gift of a book. Best of all, *A Habit Called Faith* made me eager to read the Scriptures more often, to enter more deeply into this story of redemption, and to take up this habit called faith anew."

Tish Harrison Warren, Anglican priest and author of *Liturgy of the Ordinary: Sacred Practices in Everyday Life*

"In every area of life, we know that thriving comes at the price of submitting to regular, best practices. Thriving athletes (and healthy people in general) submit to best nutrition and fitness practices, thriving musicians to best instrument and vocal practices, thriving parents and spouses to best family practices, thriving leaders to best organizational practices, and the list goes on. And yet, quite oddly, many believe—or at least *behave*—as if thriving faith is something that will just happen to us, all on its own. As with every worthwhile pursuit, a thriving and sustained faith will stand or fall on whether we submit to best *spiritual* practices. For this reason, I'm so thankful for people like Jen and for resources like *A Habit Called Faith*. Especially in an age like ours in which so many souls are languishing from passive neglect, I can't think of a more needed book."

Scott Sauls, senior pastor of Christ Presbyterian Church in Nashville, Tennessee, and author of *Jesus Outside the Lines* and *A Gentle Answer*

"Getting into genuinely life-changing habits is never easy, but with Jen Michel as a companion, embarking on regular Bible reading will become more of a burden-lifting than burden-creating practice. For all looking to start, restart, or refresh daily time with God, this is the book for you."

Sam Allberry, speaker and author of *Why Bother with Church?* and *Seven Myths about Singleness*

"Jen Pollock Michel is one of my favorite living writers. This book calls us to see knowing God as not just cerebral assent but as formation and habit, as living a life through the One who is Life. *A Habit Called Faith* will help to strengthen you when you are wavering, encourage you when you are doubting, and call you back to your life in Christ when you start to feel you are losing your way."

Russell Moore, president of the Ethics & Religious Liberty Commission of the Southern Baptist Convention

"Today the Bible is often seen as a strange artifact from the past, with Christian beliefs viewed as exotic and irrelevant. The result is that in some corners of the West, the Christian faith has not simply been rejected; it has mainly been left untried. And yet, there remains a hunger for something beyond the dominant secular story lines of our age. This means that while people sometimes sense a need for something more than the shallow scripts secularism has to offer, they are also suspicious of any attempt to dust off ancient sources that claim to be a divine guide. Jen Pollock Michel models a way forward by inviting skeptics and doubters to "come and see" that Christianity does not just claim to be true—it claims to work. But only by stepping into the Bible and trying it on can one see *if* it works. So Jen welcomes everyone to come along on a journey to *see*, not only by navigating us through the smaller biblical plotlines (in Deuteronomy and the Gospel of John) but also by winsomely mapping these within the bigger story line of the Bible and engaging with the twists and turns of our modern lives. *A Habit of Faith* is a book that believers and unbelievers alike should read—and ideally read together."

Joshua Chatraw, director of the Center for Public Christianity and author of *Telling a Better Story*

A HABIT CALLED FAITH

A HABIT CALLED FAITH

40 DAYS IN THE BIBLE
TO FIND AND FOLLOW JESUS

JEN POLLOCK MICHEL

BakerBooks
a division of Baker Publishing Group
Grand Rapids, Michigan

Published by Baker Books
a division of Baker Publishing Group
PO Box 6287, Grand Rapids, MI 49516-6287
www.bakerbooks.com

Library of Congress Cataloging-in-Publication Data
Names: Michel, Jen Pollock, 1974– author.
Title: A habit called faith : 40 days in the Bible to find and follow Jesus / Jen Pollock Michel.
Description: Grand Rapids, Michigan : Baker Books, a division of Baker Publishing Group, 2021. | Includes bibliographical references.
Identifiers: LCCN 2020035439 | ISBN 9781540900531 (paperback) | ISBN 9781540901477 (casebound)
Subjects: LCSH: Bible—Devotional literature. | Bible. Deuteronomy—Devotional literature. | Bible. John—Devotional literature. | Habit.
Classification: LCC BS491.5 .M53 2021 | DDC 242/.5—dc23
LC record available at https://lccn.loc.gov/2020035439

Some names and details have been changed to protect the privacy of the individuals involved.

The author is represented by Alive Literary Agency, www.aliveliterary.com.

21 22 23 24 25 26 27 7 6 5 4 3 2 1

To Esther, Jill, and Mabel:

Remember the blue heron—
and consider his mighty wings.
Deuteronomy 33:26

CONTENTS

ACKNOWLEDGMENTS

This book was seeded by an inconspicuous Pascal reference in Kent Annan's *Slow Kingdom Coming*. In the margin, I wrote, "Book idea?" I tracked down the reference and tucked it away for several years. Such are the methods of writers, which Margaret Atwood described in *Negotiating with the Dead*. She compared them to "the ways of the jackdaw: we steal the shiny bits and build them into the structures of our own disorderly nests."[1]

As I wrote the chapters to follow (and often despaired of the work), a friend likened me to the Israelites, wandering in the wilderness. In the final months, I prayed this verse nearly every day as a kind of liturgy: "Hear, Lord, and grant me grace. Lord, become helper to me" (Ps. 30:10, translation by Robert Alter). I count it a privilege to participate in a little bit of God's work in the world—and also to wholly depend upon his grace for doing it.

I am grateful to my agent, Lisa Jackson, who was as excited for the idea of this book as I was. I feel especially glad for her patience with my rambling Voxer messages.

I am grateful for this new partnership with the good people at Baker Books, including my editor, Rachel Jacobson.

I am grateful for my family: for my husband, Ryan, who continues to learn how to partner with me in this work. As I've finished this manuscript (and he's moved home for his own work because of COVID-19), we've played a lot of musical chairs, both of us in search of some quiet. For my children, Audrey, Nathan, Camille, Andrew, and Colin, who are becoming people I learn from and admire: I am grateful for your long-suffering at the dinner table, where I stand on my proverbial soapbox to try out book ideas. Thanks too for your input on the cover design. For our extended families, who read everything I write and make their friends read it, too: thank you for loving us so generously.

I am grateful for many at Grace Toronto Church: the pastors, staff, *Imprint* volunteers, and many friends. In this community and with these people, I'm learning to find and follow Jesus.

I am grateful for Jordan Pickering, who offered his theological expertise and ministry experience as a beta reader. His comments were invaluable.

I am grateful to David and Beth Booram, who offered up generous hospitality and space for me to write. I'll keep writing books just to have the excuse to visit them. I'm also grateful for Ken and Linda Gamble, who offered up office space for writing in the midst of a chaotic move.

I am grateful to everyone who shared their faith story with me: Ian Cusson, Kim Demchuk, Mika Edmondson, Shannon Galván, Mark Lawrence, Kevin Feiyu Li, Darius Rackus, Deborah Smith, Premi Suresh, and Sydni Willis. Every tearful conversation was a gift! I'm also grateful to many friends, who generously made connections: Kristie Anyabwile, Alonso Galván, Collin Hansen, Linda Kim, David Milroy, and Scott Sauls.

To others who offered early feedback on the first draft (Esther, Jill, and Mabel), thank you as well.

To friends like Lindsay, Olga, Ruben, Nalina, and Olivia, I'm grateful for your willingness to engage in spiritual conversations. I hope this book is one step on your own journey of finding and following Jesus.

INTRODUCTION

A Believer in Belief

"Did you know that Jen is a believer?" our host asked, turning to her husband as she bid us goodbye. Her voice was pitched with incredulity. I flushed. I didn't believe in unicorns. I believed in the risen Christ.

My husband, Ryan, and I had both been nervous about this dinner hosted by his business acquaintance. We'd worried over what to wear. In the end, after amassing a pile of rejections, Ryan had chosen a sport coat and a button-down shirt, deciding against a tie for the warm summer evening. The calculated risk proved to be exactly the right decision when our host opened the door of his sprawling penthouse. "Welcome!" he said, reaching immediately for his tie and loosening the knot. "I'm glad to be rid of this." In my belted seersucker dress, wedge sandals, and brightest shade of red lipstick, I tried effecting unimpeachable casualness.

We exchanged pleasantries and took in the panoramic view of Toronto's skyline from the floor-to-ceiling windows. A second couple arrived minutes behind us: the man in a tie, which he promptly removed after surveying the room, his wife the picture of corporate ambition in her dark suit.

Dinner was served in the dining room by two members of the household staff, and for the next couple of hours, Ryan and I mostly spectated a conversation that circled around global travel and art collected along the way. After dessert, the men split off, and the women moved into the living room. In our newly intimate circle of three, the wife of my husband's business acquaintance, a prolific author of bestselling novels, announced she'd turned in the manuscript of her next book just that morning.

"Jen, what do you do for a living?" she turned to ask. Until tonight, we knew only as much about each other as our husbands had cared to share. In fact, I had been under the impression that she funded their perch at Bay and Bloor with sales from steamy paperbacks.

"I'm a writer too," I answered, pausing in search of words. "I write books about faith, Christian faith."

The room fell awkwardly silent, as if time were needed to absorb what had sounded like a confession.

"Do you mean that you believe the Bible?" she asked, edging toward me.

"I do," I said.

"The literal Bible? Like Adam and Eve and Noah?" She wore a stunned look, as if I was about to also admit that I supported legislation for stoning adulterers and severing the hands of thieves. Until this point, I had been making a decent impression of being decent.

"I suppose we'd have to clarify what you mean by literal," I answered. It wasn't an evasion. I wanted to pique her interest, wanted it to persist long enough to discuss the Bible's marvelous complexity. Instead, her curiosity waned and I sat mute, my seemingly prehistoric strangeness exposed to view.

Foreign and Familiar

There is a persistent idea today that we've grown out of religion like a child grows out of shoes. Faith, in a scientific and secular age, seems ill-fitting and outdated. If we've discovered quarks and mapped the human genome, can't we finally be rid of primitive superstitions about God and the afterlife? People nurture real worries about taking faith too seriously—about taking the Bible too seriously. No one trusts the world in the hands of fundamentalists.

There is a sense that believers today are a curiosity, even a spectacle, and I've grown used to conversations like the one I've just described. I'm accustomed to people's visible misgivings when they discover that I'm a "believer." There is often a nervousness, a kind of palpable fear that should I be given the least encouragement, I might draw from some hidden pocket a heavy King James Bible and wield it as a weapon.

But maybe another shocking surprise about believers isn't simply our strangeness but also the striking similarity we bear to our religiously indifferent neighbors. Our lives can be as recognizable as they are alien. My husband and I are both university-educated with graduate degrees from respectable institutions. We live and work in a global city, contending with traffic and soaring real estate prices. Our children attend an international school whose student body is diverse in nationality, ethnicity, and religious belief. We are believers, yes, but we do not live on a bald patch of land in Idaho, canning peaches, wielding guns, and preparing for the apocalypse.[1]

Like many people I know, both believers and "nones,"[2] we aim to be good and do good. Still, believing doesn't make us reliable saints. We wake up anxious and irritable under Monday's dark sky. We binge-watch Netflix and avoid calling our aging parents on the weekends. We love and fight, give and hoard, serve and self-protect. When our windows are open on a breezy spring day, our neighbors hear us in all of our humanness.

We *believe*—but this is not to say we hover above our lives like angels. On the one hand, we do trust in a God so personal, so close, so intimately involved as to have accurate count, at any given moment of the day, of the hairs on our heads. On the other hand, our faith is not the same thing as ironclad certainty, impervious to honest questions. We *believe*—but this is not to say we never doubt, never demand proofs as Thomas did, the disciple who insisted on placing his hand on the wounds of the resurrected Jesus. There are days that faith comes easy, and there are days that it does not, especially when a friend lies dying, her too-young body riddled with cancer. Faith, at least as we live it, is less the picture of a glassy lake, unaffected by weather. We find it to be a flawed and human enterprise, subject to grief, to fear, to perplexity, even to anger. It can storm violently, even as faith holds.

What I'm trying to say is that believers—even religious belief itself—may be as familiar as foreign, despite our very bad press. Unlike what people often assume, faith is not a superpower. It's not a capacity for magical thinking, not a bent toward otherworldly positivity. Faith is not endowed or withheld at birth. It does not act like superstition, independent of rational thought, clinging to long lists of statistical improbabilities and Hallmark sentiments. Faith is not the stubborn insistence, contrary to hundreds of years of scientific observation, that the world is flat. Instead, faith looks a lot like the kind of belief all people practice. It is decided by reason and by emotion, by empirical experience and by gut instinct. Faith is not a rejection of evidence but a careful consideration of it, including the study of sacred texts. Faith also involves an inquiry into our collective human longings: for meaning, for justice, for hope when life trembles at the fault lines. One way of deciding for—and against—any system of ultimate commitments is by asking one simple question: Does its story make good sense of the world?[3] Though the Christian faith may not be exactly provable, I'm ready to argue that it remains an entirely defensible way of knowing. In fact, as research suggests, all knowledge is informed by what we expect to see.[4]

My question for readers is, Why not, if only for the period of forty days, expect to see God?

Going through the Motions

In *The Power of Habit*, Charles Duhigg examines the case of Eugene Pauly, who in 1993 suffered from viral encephalitis. After a ten-day coma, Pauly recovered, although he never regained memory of the previous three decades of his life. Pauly had also lost the ability to form new memories, even the memory of his illness and resulting amnesia.

When his wife, Beverly, eventually took Eugene home from the hospital, it wasn't easy for her to spend the litany of long days with him. Her husband was happy enough but also irritatingly insistent upon asking the same questions over and over again. As a distraction, the couple took walks around the block every morning and every afternoon, always following the same route. One day, Eugene slipped outside without Beverly noticing. When she finally discovered his absence, she frantically combed the neighborhood, hours later returning without Eugene and despairing for his safety. But upon opening the front door, Beverly was shocked to find Eugene sitting in the living room, watching the History Channel. Her husband had no memory of leaving the house, no memory of coming home. If asked, Eugene could never draw a map of his neighborhood. Still, it appeared that he had learned to navigate the streets, not by consciously memorizing their names, but by walking the same route, day after day. His education was an education by habit.

I want to suggest that faith can be formed in much this same way: by virtue of repetitive motion.

Seventeenth-century mathematician Blaise Pascal understood the transformative power of habit. Pascal, who converted to Christian faith in his early twenties, left behind fragments of religious reflections before his premature death at the age of thirty-nine. In one of those fragments, collected as *Pensées*, Pascal commended habit as a means of faith formation. He thought habit was especially useful advice for those who, despite intellectual assent to Christian belief, still lacked a vital sense of knowing God.

Pascal suggested that people plagued by unrelenting doubt could be helped by going through the "motions" of faith. "You want to be cured of unbelief and you ask for the remedy: learn from those who were once bound like you and now wager all they have. . . . They behaved just as if they did believe, taking holy water, having masses said, and so on. That will make you believe quite naturally."[5] Pascal's advice was intensely practical. Don't just try thinking your way into faith, he advised. Try *practicing* your way into faith. Go to church, follow the liturgy, act the part. Let habit take you by the hand and lead you to God.

There are limits, of course, to the power of habit. Repetitive motion can empty faith of its meaning and make of it something more rote than real. There is kneeling that isn't prayer, singing that isn't praise. As Jesus himself taught in the Sermon on the Mount, it is tragically possible to spend Sunday after Sunday, year after year, looking the credible part of the "believer" without ever really believing. I'm not suggesting that the motions of faith are faith itself.

Still, faith may have as much to do with habits as epiphanies.

Forty Days of Faith

When I took up faith in Jesus the summer before my junior year of high school, I took up its habits too. This wasn't my own bright idea. Someone had encouraged me to commit to forming the habits of Christian life, including the habit of reading the Bible ten minutes every day for six months. I took that advice, half-scared that if I didn't, the transformation that had started to take place in me would just as easily be uprooted. I began to read the Bible to stand on my foal legs of faith. I read it to learn to walk.

I still do.

Jesus talked about feasting on the words of God as if they were food itself. To experience Scripture as food is to feel faint and famished for its every reminder. In other words, reading the Bible regularly is a spiritual practice that has less to do with drudgery and more to do with delight. We don't need to be asked twice to eat when we're ravenously hungry—especially if the kitchen smells of freshly baked bread.

Wherever you find yourself across the spectrum of faith, whether you're more hostile or more indifferent, more curious or more convinced, I am offering to you this encouragement: the commitment to forty days of reading the Bible might open some back door of faith without you even struggling to open it. It's an ordinary habit with extraordinary results.

Am I audacious enough to hope that, in proposing this forty-course meal of Scripture, the time-pressed people of our bustling century can still themselves just long enough to linger with a very old book? I am. I recognize, of course, that taking up the habit of Scripture reading will require laying other habits down. Modern life, as we all know it, is hurried and hassled, boredom a relic of an earlier age. Today we have no real time to "kill."

But it is also important to admit—better, to *confess*—that many of us choose busy as often as busy chooses us. Maybe, in order to make room for Scripture reading, we might decide to abandon social media for a period of forty days. Maybe we'll choose to give up Netflix. Maybe we'll set our alarm thirty minutes earlier to create blank space in crowded days. Importantly, I think we'll find that the discipline will best be sustained when we do it with a friend or group of friends and keep track of our consistency.[6]

Perhaps you find yourself wishing for an easier, less strenuous method of faith formation than forty days of reading and reflection. Truthfully, I do too. It seems that with every technological advance that reduces our burden of moving through the physical world, we're left with the illusion that exertion—whether physical, emotional, intellectual, or even spiritual—is our enemy. I think it's worth hearing Jesus's paradoxical promise to those of us looking to cultivate a faith-full life: "Come to me, all who labor and are heavy laden, and I will give you rest. Take my yoke upon you, and learn from me, for I am gentle and lowly in heart, and you will find rest for your souls. For my yoke is easy, and my burden is light."[7] Jesus offers us a path to knowing God that isn't strenuous—but also not effortless. As the late Dallas Willard, a philosopher and Christian writer, often said, there's nothing accidental about the spiritual life. It requires our intention, our agency. It requires that we show up. That's what I'm asking you to do for the next forty days.

Looking back on more than twenty-five years as a Christian, I can see now how slowly, how incrementally faith grows, how its bricks are laid, one by one. This isn't something we can be impatient about, even if the labor can sometimes feel dispiritingly tedious. We must learn to keep at it, remembering that Jesus said the strongest houses are built by hearing the words of God.

The great promise is this: in days of storm, that house stands.

I can say plainly that the life of faith is a good one; it is, as we'll see in the readings to come, *life*. I do not feign indifference to whether people are moved closer to faith in Jesus Christ at the end of this experiment because I am not indifferent. I hope every faith story that I've chosen to include, along with the daily readings, will invite readers to see the varied ways God calls people to find and follow Jesus. Neither, however, am I tied up in knots about the consequential decisions people could make at the end of a book like this. To choose for or against faith is, paradoxically, a response to the initiative of God. As we will see from our readings ahead, the God of the Bible is a God who seeks and saves the lost. He risks the flock to rescue the stray. We may feel ourselves to be fumbling in the dark, holding out weak hope for finding God. We may feel as if our insistent "Marco" waits interminably on God's faint "Polo." But the truth is greater, grander, and more grace-filled than such hide-and-seek imaginings. His words whisper with the wind. We need only ask for ears to hear, eyes to see, and hearts to understand.

A NOTE TO THE READER

To orient you to the pages ahead, this book is divided into forty daily readings, each with an assigned passage of Scripture, a shorter selection of verses, my reflection, and two questions.

If you already have an established habit of daily prayer and Scripture reading, you might choose to read the assigned chapter of Scripture in its entirety as well as the reflection that I've written. If you're just beginning to practice this habit of faith, you may opt instead for the shorter selection of verses in addition to the daily reflection. Either way, plodding along at an average pace, you should be finished in the time it takes to watch an episode of your favorite show.

There are some natural "beginnings" in the year that lend themselves to starting new habits like this one: a new calendar year, a new school year, or a sacred season in the church calendar, such as Lent. It's not necessary to do the forty days of reading in forty days, but research suggests that habits are best formed by daily practice.[1] Try for regularity in your readings!

If you're reading on your own, I hope you'll consider journaling your answers to each day's reflection questions. We think better with a pen in our hand. I'd encourage you also to try wrangling a friend into this forty-day journey with you. Accountability will keep you going.

If you're using this book in a group study, I suggest dividing the readings into an eight-week study and using the discussion guide at the back of this book. If some group members find it difficult to commit to all forty of the daily readings, I've noted in parentheses an accelerated way through the book's content.

Week 1: Introduction, Days 1–5 (Days 1, 5)
Week 2: Days 6–10 (Days 6, 9)
Week 3: Days 11–15 (Days 11, 15)
Week 4: Days 16–20 (Days 16, 20)
Week 5: Days 21–25 (Days 21, 23)
Week 6: Days 26–30 (Days 26, 30)
Week 7: Days 31–35 (Days 31, 34)
Week 8: Days 36–40, Epilogue (Days 38, 39)

The most important piece of advice I have for you is this: *finish*. I was reminded about the power of "finishing" at a recent panel discussion that our church hosted for writers, artists, and musicians in our congregation. Canadian composer Ian Cusson, whose faith story is featured in this book, was asked what advice he'd give to his younger creative self. "Finish," he said. He emphasized how many of the real lessons of "making" were hard-won in the latter half of any particular project.

That rings true to me for this endeavor too. The real reward will be in the finishing.

MARK LAWRENCE

"God, I don't know if you exist,
but I'm going to act like you do."

Mark Lawrence was born into a Methodist family in 1950. His only habits of faith were church attendance and Sunday School. "I can't really say it took root," he explained. In his early years at California State University, he dated a girl who professed to be a Christian, though she eventually broke off the relationship because of their faith differences. "That set me on a search."

Mark's spiritual curiosities were stoked by readings assigned for an undergraduate philosophy course, especially the writings of Christian existentialist Søren Kierkegaard. The following fall, Mark took a backgrounds in literature class in which he traversed the Western canon and appreciated, for the first time, the considerable influence of Christianity on the West's literary heritage. He recalled the day the professor had announced a test on John Calvin's doctrine of the sovereignty of God. "I reread [Calvin's work] with the expectation that I would go into the class and argue against the sovereignty of God. But once I started writing, I unexpectedly defended it."

Intellectually, Mark had begun to assent to vague notions of God's existence, which he defended one day to his friend, an atheist majoring in religion. As they argued, both noticed a small crowd gathering around a man, Bible in hand, who had begun to preach at the center of the campus quad. He was met with jeers and ridicule. "It was as if my eyes were opened," Mark remembered. "I saw this response of the average, secular college student in 1971 as they became rapidly angry. I thought, *Isn't this odd? Someone can come on the college campus and talk about Marxism, Hinduism, Buddhism, anything you could imagine, and there would not be this kind of antagonism.*"

Mark continued to follow his spiritual curiosities through the reading of other philosophical works, returning home to "the usual family dysfunction" for the Thanksgiving holiday. On Thursday evening, Mark left the house for a pensive walk. Time collapsed, and suddenly Mark found himself inexplicably on his knees, praying: "God, I don't know if you exist, but I'm going to act as if you do." When he returned home around 10:00 p.m., he was met by a ringing phone; friends wanted him to join them at a local bar. Having forgotten the prayer he'd just prayed, he said yes and hung up the phone. Then, remembering his prayer, he was faced with an ethical choice. His older brother, recently estranged from his wife and living with his parents who'd been working hard to keep him sober (he'd been struggling with addictions to LSD and heroin), asked to tag along, prompting a family argument. That's when Mark heard a voice within him, new and yet recognizable. "Mark, you have watched your brother on this self-destructive path, and you've never once stepped into this dysfunction." Realizing the voice likely belonged to God, Mark obeyed. "I entered into the situation. I said to my brother, 'I've been watching you destroy yourself for well over ten years, and I've never said anything. The reality is you are lying to Mom and Dad. You're still taking drugs, and they haven't the slightest idea of what you're up to. Unless you get yourself some help, I'm not going to stay in this house one night longer.'" A three-hour heated conversation ensued, and Mark eventually left with his sleeping bag to sleep in a nearby field. He spent the rest of the weekend reading the four biographies of Jesus in the New Testament.

Back on campus, Mark was plunged into doubt over his newfound faith—if it could yet be called faith. As he walked to class one day, he prayed, "God, this whole thing seems like a big cosmic myth to me. You'd better do something soon, or I'm going to throw the whole thing out the window." No sooner had he finished praying his "deep faith-filled prayer" than he saw a sign on a college bulletin board advertising a revival. "Well, if I've already crucified my intellect in becoming a Christian, I may as well go all the way." He wrote down the address, which took him, later that evening, into an inner-city section of Sacramento and to a storefront church called Apostolic Church of the Holy Christ, Jesus Christ Our Ebenezer. He was standing out front when an African American woman drove up, explaining that the revival wouldn't start for another hour but that he could wait at the minister's house next door. Once the service began, Mark learned, as the same woman sat on the front row, rocking back and forth, her body occasionally jolting and her arms flying up in the air, that she was the evangelist leading the revival. Watching her movements, Mark concluded, *That must be the Holy Ghost I've been reading about in the book of Acts.*

People began to pile into the church, and the night unfurled with long stretches of preaching and singing, preaching and singing. As one hour gave way to another and another, the evangelist eventually announced, "Some young man shouldn't leave here before he's baptized in the Holy Ghost." To Mark's surprise, an elderly gentleman of nearly eighty slipped from his pew and made it to the front. The woman touched his forehead, and his weak legs gave way to dancing. "I heard the inner voice tell me to get in line." But Mark was skeptical. *If she touches me and nothing happens, I won't be able to dance like that*, Mark mused, letting his doubt trail off.

He reached the front. The evangelist touched him lightly on the forehead. Mark fell immediately to the floor. *Mark*, he said to himself, *there is no rational reason why you should be on the floor. Get up*. Mark got up, then fell again, his legs wobbly and weak beneath him. This time, it was the poetry of John Donne that echoed in his head: "Whom the Lord raises up, he first throws down."[1] Donne's verse was followed by the voice that had been speaking to him since he'd knelt in the blackness of that Thanksgiving night: *Mark, you won't be able to stand up until you're willing to stand up totally with Jesus*. He got up and was baptized that night. Relaying the details of his story later to a Christian minister on campus, the man was skeptical. "It didn't fit his template. He had a template of what the Christian life was like.

"Ironically, that was part of what kept me from the Christian life."

The Rt. Rev. Mark J. Lawrence is Bishop, The Anglican Diocese of South Carolina.

DAY 1

Read: Deuteronomy 1:1–5 (Focus: vv. 1–5)

Key Verse: "These are the words that Moses spoke to all Israel beyond the Jordan in the wilderness." (v. 1)

Lend Me Your Ears

One year after I graduated from college and started teaching high school, I began a master's degree in literature. I hadn't wanted to return to school so soon, but my department chair, rubbing his tired eyes and nodding at the framed picture of his two young children on his desk, warned it would never get easier.

My first course was Victorian literature. It was taught by a short, balding man, uniformed every week in Converse high tops and tight, cuffed jeans. After I missed the first lecture, he called to inform me that I'd missed the sign-ups for the two required course presentations. I was expected to deliver both upon my return: a ten-page close reading of Charles Dickens's novel, *Bleak House*, and a ten-page essay on Jacques Derrida.

I've spent much of my formal education studying books. And despite how obvious it sounds, the Bible is a book—or, more accurately put, a book of books, authored across many centuries by different authors, all of them moved by the steady rhythm of God's whisper. Christians believe the Bible is a God-breathed book.

Today, we read from the opening verses of the book of Deuteronomy. Its English title derives from the Greek *Deuteronomium*; its Hebrew title, *Devarim*, owes to its opening phrase in verse 1:

"These are the words."[1] Deuteronomy is a collection of sermons preached by Moses to the nation of Israel forty years after the exodus, when God's people were delivered out of slavery in Egypt. It is both a record of Moses's words and a record of God's words, "given in commandment" to Israel.

These first five verses of Deuteronomy situate us in the setting of our story: the who, where, and when. But we would be wrong to read these verses simply as an introduction. In fact, "these are the words" underscores a central theological point of Deuteronomy. This opening phrase tells us something of the nature of God as well as something of the imperative of faith. "These are the words" insists that there is a God, and that he speaks. They insist that in order to be his people, we must cultivate the habit of good listening.

Given the scale of our universe (and the unknown universes beyond), it should not seem at all self-evident that God, if he *is*, should also *speak* to his people. What right do any of us have to presume God's interest in our ant-sized lives? When we think of the God who created and sustains all things, it is easy to see how he might have chosen to shroud himself in mystery and impenetrable obscurity. But the Bible tells us that while he is transcendent and holy, he also parted the clouds to speak. In fact, this was one of his first great acts of love: his decision to speak.

Deuteronomy assumes our familiarity with the speaking God of Genesis, who spoke the world into being and called one man, Abraham, to follow him.[2] It assumes our familiarity with the events at Horeb, or Mount Sinai, where God condescended in a cloud to speak to the nation of Israel—this extended family of Abraham—whom he had rescued from their slavery in Egypt.[3] When many years earlier, Moses had asked to catch a glimpse of him, God had refused to show his face and instead had spoken his name aloud to Moses: "The LORD, the LORD, a God merciful and gracious, slow to anger, and abounding in steadfast love and faithfulness, keeping steadfast love for thousands, forgiving iniquity and transgression and sin."[4] God's speaking reveals God's goodness—especially because, as we'll soon learn, God's people are tragically hard of hearing.

The speaking God of Deuteronomy is a God of grace. We aren't usually accustomed to thinking of him like this. As early as the second century, some Christians began to argue that the church would be better off to dispense with the Old Testament in favor of the New. Admittedly, these opening verses in Deuteronomy confront us with the difficulty of reading this ancient book. Who is this God who "struck down" ancient kings and displaced peoples to give his own people their land?

As careful readers of the Bible, we want to raise and address these important questions. We can't gloss over difficulties in the text, pretending the road is paved rather than potholed. We'll have to take curves slowly. We'll have to admit what makes us squirm. The Bible can't always be cut from felt and dramatized on flannelgraph. It will not baptize our preferences or bow to our biases. According to Deuteronomy, Moses's words are not merely human words but binding words, given by God in the form of a "commandment." They bear down on us with authority, and it will not be we who judge them but they who judge us. If God *is* and God *speaks*, as the people who belong to him, it is incumbent on us to hear.

As a child, when my brother and I weren't listening very well, my father would playfully assume an imperious tone and hold an imaginary bag to the sides of our heads, citing Shakespeare: "Friends, Romans, Countrymen, lend me your ears!"[5] Strangely, it's this line I hear in my head as I open these first five verses of the book named, "These are the words." I find myself wondering about this habit of "lending our ears," and I think of Jesus, who ended many of his own sermons with a similar plea: "He who has ears, let him hear."

To think that faith might be owed to something as simple as ears.

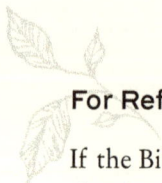

For Reflection/Discussion

If the Bible is the record of God's words to his people (and not simply a flawed human artifact), how might this change the way you read it? What is one practical way you can cultivate the habit of listening to God in your life?

DAY 2

Read Deuteronomy 1:6–46 (Focus: vv. 26–33)

Key Verse: "Yet in spite of this word you did not believe the Lord *your God." (v. 32)*

Oh, the Places You'll Go

With Toronto finally thawing as I write, my eighty-year-old neighbor spends the days gardening. This morning, I looked out my front yard to find Sue bent over the dandelions. I crossed the street, intending to say a quick hello, but she was determined to show me the blooming green of her backyard.

"That's the garlic," Sue said, pointing beyond the clothesline to a small garden plot behind some chicken wire. She then led me to the trellis close to the house, lamenting that the clematis, a thick, white canopy last summer, was relatively barren this year. I listened to Sue complain about the vagrant groundhog who returns, spring after spring, to eat her garden vegetables. Sue has spent more than six decades on this block, and this place has borne witness to her life and to her family's story.

The story of the Bible, like the story of Sue and her family, is also bound up in the geographical setting. It's a story of place as well as a story of people. As the book of Deuteronomy opens, we see that God's people are not yet rooted in the land of Canaan, promised many generations earlier to Abraham, Isaac, and Jacob. They are, of all seemingly godforsaken places, east of the Jordan river.[1] In a very real sense, they are standing outside the promises of

God, their noses pressed to the glass, the glass fogged with longing. To be "beyond the Jordan in the wilderness" is our narrative hint that something has gone terribly wrong. Though God's people had been delivered from Egyptian slavery forty years earlier, we now understand that they have been catastrophically detoured. This makes the story of Deuteronomy the story of an in-between place. Isn't that where we need faith the most?

Two significant places mentioned in today's reading help us understand some of the winding, wandering journey that Israel has been on. The first place is Horeb, or Mount Sinai. In the story of Israel, Mount Sinai is more than a geographical high point in the wilderness landscape. In terms of literary structure, some scholars would say that the biblical story climbs and descends from this mountain where Moses receives the Ten Commandments, or ten words, of God.[2]

In addition to Sinai, the second place bearing witness to Israel's story, according to today's reading, is Kadesh Barnea. Upon arriving at this southern outpost after their journey from Egypt, God's people decided to send twelve spies to scout out the promised land. This physical "seeing" of the land should have reminded them of all they'd already "seen" of God's protection, provision, and power. They'd *seen* God's power when he delivered them out of Egypt; they'd *seen* God leading them, by fire and cloud, through the wilderness. Their physical *seeing* of God acting on their behalf was meant as antecedent for the *seeing* of faith that was now required at the edge of the promised land: "See, I have set the land before you. Go in and take possession of [it]." But at Kadesh Barnea, Israel miserably failed that test of faith.

The spies returned from the reconnaissance mission with succulent fruit, its juices staining their hands, but the bounty of the land did not prevent their terror. The land was good, ten of the spies conceded, but surely God was not. At Kadesh Barnea, they spun an unrecognizable story—how God hated them, how he had brought them out of the land of Egypt in order to destroy them. Fear played tricks with memory.

These two places—Mount Sinai and Kadesh Barnea—call to mind one of the earliest places in the Bible: the garden of Eden. Like my neighbor Sue, God had planted and tended a garden for his people. But in the third chapter of Genesis, Adam and Eve rejected the words of God and despised the fruit of this promised land, a bounty that had been provided to them by his good hands. He'd given every tree for their sustenance, forbidding only one. But when an enemy slithered into their garden home to cast suspicion on the words of God and to tempt them to take what God had withheld, Eve was seduced by this question: "Did God really say?"

We never imagine our refusal to hear and obey God's words as ruinous as it always turns out to be. But when Israel rejected the words of God, despising the blessing he held out to them, God in turn rejected their words. Though they made hasty, superficial apologies, presumptively trying to change course, God judged their rebellion and sentenced an entire generation to die in the wilderness. Kadesh Barnea is a place that signals a dramatic failure of faith—a failure of which we are all capable.

This is all to say: when we turn the pages of the Bible, we don't glimpse saintly and self-sacrificing people, punctilious in their rule following. The characters in the Bible are not the haloed, unreal figures of medieval paintings. They are full of foibles, beset by fear, victim to the inescapable, unrelenting frailty that is humanness. They can't keep sight of God. Israel is no exemplar in the life of faith; she is as ruined as we feel ourselves to be.

Places like Horeb and Kadesh Barnea remind us of the kind of story the Bible is trying to tell. It emphatically rejects the mode of the epic and its inimitable heroes. Instead, the Bible favors stories thick with humanity: not people as they wish themselves to be, but people as they really are. It is in this reality, and nowhere else, that God must find—and save—all of us.

It is not always our habit to lend our ears to God. It is also our habit to plug them.

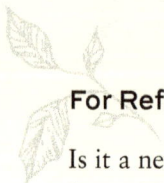

For Reflection/Discussion

Is it a new insight for you to learn that the Bible isn't a book of heroes? What might we expect to find in the Bible if it's not perfect moral examples to imitate?

DAY 3

Read Deuteronomy 2:1–37 (Focus: vv. 1–8)

Key Verse: "These forty years the Lord *your God has been with you. You have lacked nothing." (v. 7)*

Mirror, Mirror, on the Wall

My mother stayed nearly two weeks after I had my first baby. I was a typically anxious new mother. I paged furiously through books for reasons why the baby wasn't sleeping. My mother, on the other hand, was decisive and calm, and I marveled at her heroism of single-handedly managing the baby *and* dinner. When she and my stepfather pulled out of my driveway at the end of their visit, I stood crying at the front window, dressed in my pajamas.

Growing up, I'd always seen myself as the principal character in life's drama. Only later, after my foray into motherhood, did my own mother emerge as more than a supporting actor in my story. It was an obvious reminder of one of the basic lessons of adulthood: it's not all about you.

This too is a lesson of faith. As we read the Bible, we discover the kind of story it has to tell—and we discover that God is at the very center of that story. The Bible is God-centric in its every impulse: "In the beginning, *God*."[1] When we open the Bible, we should expect to see God.

Still, a paradox unfolds between the pages of Genesis and Revelation. For as much as God's book is about God, we can't help discovering ourselves in its pages: the fears that paralyze us, the greed that corrupts us, the worries that whisper under cover of dark. If the Bible is a window for rightly seeing God, it is also a mirror for soberly seeing ourselves.

Strikingly, God's book makes a meticulous, sometimes somnolent record of human history. As we learn in our reading today, nothing has been accidental about Israel's wilderness itinerary. God shepherded this teeming multitude of men, women, children, and livestock from place to place. He indicated where to stop, how long to stay, when to depart, and what direction to travel. He pledged himself to accompany this small nation. He promised to *be with* them. This doesn't put Israel at the center of the story, but it does remind us that God's love is personal, that his love demands an object.

The God of the Bible is bent on company.

Nevertheless, some might read this book and accuse God's love of being tribal. With only a cursory glance through Deuteronomy, some readers might perceive God's love as sheltering the few while abandoning the many. Deuteronomy could carelessly be read as an ethnocentric account of one nation dispossessing others. Worse, it could be mistakenly read as the story of divinely sanctioned violence: one nation brandishing God's favor as rationale for bloodthirsty slaughter. It might prove to be Exhibit A in the case against religion and its inevitable sectarianism.

This would be to commit several critical errors. First, the God of Deuteronomy does not declare himself to be a tribal god with regionally limited power. He is not simply Lord over Israel; he is Lord of heaven and earth. Second, to accuse the God of Israel of tribalism would be to ignore Israel's founding story. When God called Abraham to belong to him, he intended to extend his love to the entire human race. Israel would be God's holy city set on a hill, their light spilling out to illuminate the whole darkened world.[2] The love story of the Bible is missional, moving outward and reaching far.

If God's love were a tribal affair, we'd expect to see divine favor exclusively reserved for Israel—and curse reserved for everyone else. There would be predictable winners and losers in this game. But today's reading subverts that expectation. In fact, we know from chapter 1 that God has rained judgment on his own people, ensuring that an entire generation of rebels dies in the wilderness rather than inherit the promised land. By contrast, in chapter 2, God protects Moab, the very people whose king had, years earlier, bribed a prophet to rain curses upon Israel.[3] He protects the people of Edom, or Mount Seir, these outcast descendants of Jacob's twin brother, Esau, who sold his birthright and was cheated of the firstborn blessing.[4] He forbids war with the Ammonites, descendants of Lot, the nephew who set out with his uncle Abraham many years earlier to the land God had promised.[5] Much to our surprise, God's blessing is prodigally and liberally cast beyond the borders of Israel.

This is not to ignore the fact that the cities of Heshbon are wiped out, and men, women, and children die.[6] It is, however, to ask this important question: Is this the only thing about the Bible to outrage and offend? Even if the Bible avoided scenes of bloodshed, might we find other reasons to hold its words in contempt? How easily do we submit to the words of God when it requires us to forgive, even to forgive someone who refuses to offer an apology? What do we do with the Bible's call to humility rather than self-promotion, even if it means forfeiting well-deserved credit? How do we react when the Bible confronts our habits of consumption, calling us to live less extravagantly than the Joneses? To be honest, the Bible's offenses are legion—in the New Testament just as well as in the Old.

I became a follower of Jesus at the age of sixteen. Though I'd religiously attended church all of my childhood and memorized all of the Sunday School answers about God, I had, until then, no intention to stop sleeping with my boyfriend. When I became a

Christian, however, I started to read the Bible and understand the real claims God was making on my life. The Bible did not always say what I wanted it to say; it did not always approve what I wanted it to approve. It introduced a God whose ways were not my ways, whose thoughts were not my thoughts, and that was an exercise both terrifying and comforting. As I began to understand, a god in my own image was no God at all. Faith involved the habit of hearing God's words—and also the habit of feeling their weight.

There is often a chafing that happens when we read the Bible. We uncover our resistance to God's authority. However, the good news is that we can become the kind of people who trust the words of God and learn to gladly obey them.

The good news is that faith can start to hurt a little less.

For Reflection/Discussion

Before you began reading Deuteronomy, what kind of God did you expect to find in its pages? In what ways are your expectations of God (and the Bible) being confirmed or challenged?

DAY 4

Read Deuteronomy 3:1–29 (Focus: vv. 23–29)

Key Verses: "And I pleaded with the Lord *at that time, saying, '. . . Please let me go over and see the good land.'" (vv. 23, 25)*

No Do-Over

One of our five children has mastered the virtue (vice?) of persistence. On the days when I'm feeling generous and this child pleads for more screen time, more orange juice, and another episode of our favorite cooking show, delaying bedtime another half hour, I say a sunny, breezy yes. On other days, when clouds of irritability unexpectedly move in on me, this same child pleads for those same privileges—and I say an emphatic, capricious no. It's then that the real lawyerly argumentation begins. I say it more forcefully, more loudly. Still, he is the tide, and I am the cliff. My resistance erodes.

This indefatigable quality will either get our son thrown in jail—or possibly elected to political office.

In our reading today, Moses has assumed the courage to plead with God, but God has proven more intractable than me. The divine no remains no. Though Moses has spent the last forty years faithfully carrying the burden of God's complaining people, he will not enter Canaan because of his sin. In his place, Joshua, one of the two faithful spies of the twelve who were sent, will carry the torch of leadership across the Jordan and settle the people into the land.[1]

Much of the Pentateuch is taken up with the story of Moses's life, this Jewish man raised by an Egyptian princess.[2] The book of Genesis, which spans two thousand years of history before Moses's birth, accounts for only one-quarter of the Pentateuch. By contrast, Exodus through Deuteronomy, which spans only the 120-year lifetime of Moses, nevertheless accounts for three-quarters of its material. Given this analysis of literary real estate, it's easy to surmise that these first five books are a work of biography as much as a work of theology, and we might easily mistake Moses for the main character.

But this would be to forget a previous lesson, which reminded us that the Bible is God's book—and God's story. As we turn its pages, we look to grow in understanding of God's character: how he loves, why he forgives, what he promises. Today, as we eavesdrop on Moses's prayer, we discover something of God's mercy: God *listens*, bending his ear to the earth to receive the pleas of his people. It may not be that God answers every prayer we ask, as with Moses, but it can always be our confidence that he hears. It's why one important habit of faith is talking to him.

For the nation of Israel, Deuteronomy represents a redemptive moment. Though the parents of the Deuteronomic generation had cowered and refused to enter the land for fear of its fortified cities and towering inhabitants, forty years later, when their children faced these same obstacles, they trusted the words of God and marched toward military victory. Two kingdoms fell east of the Jordan River, foreshadowing more military success ahead in Canaan.

Moses, however, is not granted the privilege of the entire nation. There will be no do-over for him. If I'm honest, I have to admit that I wrestle with the perceived injustice of God's harshness. I want a dispensation of mercy for Moses. I want God to concede that while Moses's leadership was far from perfect, it was a lot more commendable than the constant whining of Israel. I want

God to feel a little more good humor. I want his mood to lighten, want to hear him reassure Moses that he sympathized with the difficulty of the job with which he was tasked. I want him to remember how Moses had even tried to refuse that task, citing his own inability.[3] I want God to weigh Moses in the balance, and I want to see the scales tipped in favor of Moses's faithfulness. I guess what I really want is for God to give some credit to Moses for trying—and to reassure me that he isn't someday going to be angry and unforgiving with me.

This story might have us wondering about God's capriciousness. Maybe God, like me, has his sunny and cloudy days. But the story line of the Bible convinces me otherwise, especially in anticipation of our study of John. In the life of Moses, God's anger is not cruelly poured out in order to prove his divine heavyweight status. It's not a thunderclap of fickleness, not a lightning strike of divine whim. Although not a perfect parallel, when God judges Moses, it seems to foreshadow the greater event of the cross of Jesus Christ—where God sentences the one in favor of acquitting the many. If Israel gets a blessing they haven't deserved, we could call that grace.

I don't like the answer that Moses gets from God, but I like knowing that Moses felt it was possible to plead with God in this way. I like that he dares to bring his honest desires into conversation with God, that he models a habit of faith that is more than the stiff upper lip and the brave face. He practices vulnerability and risk. I like knowing that while God doesn't grant Moses exactly what he asks, he is nonetheless moved by his plea. Moses is not permitted to enter the land, but he is invited to climb Mount Pisgah and glimpse God's goodness from its heights.

God hears every prayer that we pray. And even if he does not give us what we ask for, we can be assured that he will give us what we would have asked for had we had his wisdom.[4] As Jesus taught his disciples, God is not a father who gives a serpent when his son asks for a fish, nor a scorpion when his son asks for an egg.[5] Even when we aren't sure about the "rightness" of our requests, learning from Moses's example, we can bring them to God and let him do the proper vetting.

Whatever we have from his hand, we can practice the habit of trusting that it's good.

For Reflection/Discussion

How does this story inform the way that you view prayer? How would you like to begin or deepen your own habit of talking to God?

DAY 5

Read Deuteronomy 4:1–49 (*Focus: vv. 32–40*)

Key Verse: "For what great nation is there that has a god so near to it as the Lord *our God is to us, whenever we call upon him?"* (*v. 7*)

To Have and to Hold

I've been sleeping with the same man for twenty-three years. We met in college and married at twenty-two. Together, we've managed growing up, graduate school, the building of our careers, the building of a family, including the surprise addition of twins to our then-fulsome family of five. There has been more health than sickness—even if at thirty, Ryan was diagnosed with Type 1 diabetes. There has been more richer than poorer—even if we, too, have worried about getting our children through college. There has been more better than worse—even if, like every marriage, we wake up to each other's chronic sameness. In the sometimes-tired familiarity of marriage, there are yet glimpses of miracles—namely, the miracle that we keep keeping at it. We keep choosing to have and to hold. I marvel at the ordinary, marvelous work of attempting to keep these promises till the parting of death. I remember how much sustaining grace is required every day.

"You've never met an idea you don't like," Ryan once told me. And he's right: I don't really know how to love long. I am a dilettante at heart. This may be why I find the word *covenant* in the Bible so appealing.[1] Covenant, a word that broadly describes ancient contracts and agreements, treaties and alliances, signals the kind of promises God makes and the kind of promises God keeps: the unwavering, enduring, unconditional kind. It's a word that signals that God's word is his bond.

Scholars have noted the similarity between the covenant outlined in the book of Deuteronomy and in ancient Near Eastern treaties. In Deuteronomy, we discover what it means to serve God the King and to belong to him. In Deuteronomy 4, we're reminded that God made a covenant with his people at the blazing foot of Mount Sinai when he thundered his word to Israel. This Sinai covenant echoed with the memory of an earlier covenant "cut" with Abraham and dramatized in Genesis 15 when, at dusk, Abraham fell into a deep sleep and God spoke words of promise to him.[2] God said that the aged man would become the father of a nation that would suffer greatly before finally inheriting their forever home. It was a covenant signed, sealed, and delivered by God, Abraham having no active agency in its ratification. This man from Ur did not promise to live up to God's expectations, did not insist on making God proud. There was no spitting into palms, no signing with blood, no shaking on the pledge of mutual loyalty. The covenant was a lopsided promise, the weight of it resting fully on God and his promise keeping. The covenant was ratified while Abraham slept like a baby.

By contrast, the people at Sinai were not asleep but awake, terrified by the blazing, burning holiness of God. God set before them the stipulations of the covenant, that they were a people called to obey his word, and the grace of the covenant was as evident to them as it was to Abraham. It was God who condescended to his people, God who revealed his will to his people—and most importantly, God who promised to remain faithful in spite of Israel's future faithlessness. Israel would be a people who failed the covenant, who forgot the goodness of God and chased after lesser things, realizing their stupidity far too late—after home was mostly memory. Their sin was not inconsequential; it would result in exile. But a return to God, and a renewal of the covenant, promised always to be possible: because God had committed himself to forbear and to forgive. Israel would be the unfaithful wife, but God would be the devoted husband. The covenant was guaranteed by the goodness of God.

Think about this, Moses says to Israel, asking the people to consider what god is like the God of Israel, whose power and presence they have witnessed and by whose mighty hand and outstretched arm they have been delivered. He wants them to understand that faith is not cause but effect, not call but response: a response to the God whose love sets everything into motion. We don't love God in order to be loved by him. We love God because he first loved us.[3] And just as God's love for his people isn't expressed in the abstract, neither is our love for God. "Therefore you shall keep his statutes and his commandments, which I command you today, that it may go well with you and with your children after you, and that you may prolong your days in the land that the LORD your God is giving you for all time." To love God is to obey him—because the commands of God are not simply for us to *know* but to *do*.

When we find ourselves wondering about the connection between the Old and New Testaments, it's the theme of covenant that ties the two together. God's love and promise keeping are the sustaining force of the entire biblical narrative. I like how another scholar explores the paradox of the biblical covenant, that "divine freedom and divine self-obligation are held together in this single word [of covenant]." Because of his own character, God is obligated to keep his word to Israel. He cannot—must not—fail any of his promises. At the same time, God is as free as he is bound, and it is his "ever new . . . decision . . . to continue to honor that commitment."[4] Like a faithful husband, God will keep at the having and the holding of his dilettante people. Because he is faithful, fidelity is both his obligation and choice.

When I first became a Christian, I used to imagine that my connection to God was as tenuous as my feeble grip. I tried holding fast with a strict regimen of spiritual habits (prayer, Bible study, church attendance), but it always seemed that my fingers were slipping. I worried about my predilection for failing my promises rather than keeping them. Only years later did I realize that it wasn't, in fact, my grip that mattered.

As another habit of faith, I had to believe I was held fast in his strong hand.

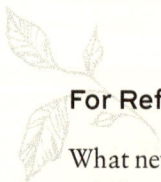

For Reflection/Discussion

What new insight have you gained about the love of God through this discussion of covenant? What keeps you from believing that God could love you in this way?

IAN CUSSON

"This is real. This is truth. I don't have any rational way of explaining why this is real and true except that it is."

Ian Cusson grew up in a Métis family off the coast of Georgian Bay in Ontario. The Métis people, born from strategic economic intermarriages of Europeans and various First Nations, settled largely in Manitoba and Ontario. His parents had very strong ties to Roman Catholicism, although their individual recollections of the church differed. His father remembered the large family Bible, which the children were forbidden to touch. "It was almost as if the power was in the physical pages." Ian's father also had recalled the strictness of the nuns at the Catholic school he attended and the rented church pews, which his family could not afford. "His experience of church was not having full access to it." Ian's mother, who had grown up in a large Catholic family as the oldest of seven kids, also attended church as a grounding part of her family's weekly routine. Ian said, "Much of how [my parents] understood life was mapped out by the church: baptism, marriage, Sunday mass, funeral, and death. How it had implications for the rest of life was another thing."

As infants, Ian and his sister were baptized into the Catholic Church, a ritual that held the utmost sacred significance. "It was the washing of your sins." His family also attended mass weekly. "It was a resetting—in terms of being good with God—although once Sunday was done, you were good to go." Ian was an altar boy as a child, and his childhood faith was simple but earnest. "I've always had a clear sense that God was real, was there. There was never a moment when I denied or questioned God's existence." However, by the time Ian turned thirteen, he had tired of what had come to feel like a perfunctory ritual. He told his mother that he no longer wanted to go to church; his sister and father soon followed suit. Still, he continued to occasionally pray throughout his teenage years. "I can remember distinct moments of crying out to God and saying to him, 'I need you, I need you, I need you.'"

At seventeen, Ian graduated from high school and earned a spot to study piano performance at the Glenn Gould School in Toronto. "There, I started asking all the big questions of life: Who is God? What does any of this mean for my life? What is the purpose of this life?" Several of the close friends he'd made at GGS were Christians who entertained Ian's questions and made themselves available for conversation over milkshakes in Toronto's Yorkville neighborhood. Once, a friend had been audacious enough to offer Ian a Bible. "Hey, you've talked a lot about life," she said. "Have you ever read the Bible?" To Ian's complete surprise (and a fair bit of consternation), she produced a copy from her backpack. "I have an extra one, and I don't need it. Do you want it?"

"I went home to my apartment and cracked open to [the Gospel of] Matthew." Normally, Ian's days were swallowed in long solitary stretches in various practice rooms at GGS; his nights were filled with echoey silences in his apartment where he lived alone. But it was in that quiet season of loneliness that Ian dedicated himself to reading the Bible. As he read through Matthew, he was struck by one phrase in particular. "I kept reading this refrain, 'weeping and gnashing of teeth.' That terrified me. I thought, *This is something that I would never in a million years want. I don't want that. I really, really don't want that.*" He finished the entire Gospel of Matthew and continued with the book that followed. "I only got into a few chapters of Mark when I remember having a moment and thinking, *This is real. This is truth. I don't have any rational way of explaining why this is real and true except that it is.*" It was a "defining moment," Ian said, one followed by his friends' invitation to attend a downtown Toronto church with them. Ian remembered that his faith continued to grow when he began attending Saturday night gatherings for young adults. Over the next year, he met weekly with a master of divinity student from Wycliffe College, who patiently answered his theological questions.

Being a Christ-follower—and Métis—is far from obvious, Ian explained. "In a complex way, I often feel like I walk in two worlds." In indigenous communities in Canada, there is deep skepticism of the church, especially when one considers the Canadian history of residential schools. "Church is equated very simplistically with a place of abuse. Church is a place of removal of culture. It's an expression of Western colonial patriarchy." Ian hopes to be a bridge for correcting some of these misconceptions, both of indigeneity and Christianity.

Ian Cusson is a composer of art song, opera, and orchestral work. Of Métis and French-Canadian descent, he explores in his work the hybridity of mixed-race identity and the intersection of Western and indigenous cultures.

DAY 6

Read Deuteronomy 5:1–33 (Focus: vv. 1–21)

Key Verse: "Hear, O Israel, the statutes and the rules that I speak in your hearing today, and you shall learn them and be careful to do them." (v. 1)

The Moment Called Now

My father was a healthy man when he died suddenly, two days after his forty-ninth birthday. I was eighteen. People lined up at the church to convey their condolences for the loss of someone so young, and at the time, I found it strange that they described my balding father in this way. Now that I'm almost that age, I feel grateful they insisted on his youth. At forty-five, I don't want to concede that time is slipping through my fingers. I don't like admitting that time, like a rationed resource, is growing scarce. When we sent our oldest daughter off to college this last fall, I held the image in my mind of a burnished oak dropping her leaves—and felt admonished for thinking that it would always be spring.

There is grief wrapped up in the human experience of time. God, of course, stands outside the limits of temporal human experience, and this makes it possible, in Deuteronomy, for time to be something pliable, something relative. In fact, the moment of greatest importance in this book is the moment called *now*. In Deuteronomy 5, for example, Moses addresses the people of Israel not as if they were the squirmy children of the lost generation but as their parents and grandparents, who had stood forty years earlier at the foot of Mount Sinai and heard the audible words of God. "The Lord spoke with *you*" (emphasis added), as if to insist they'd been witnesses to the thunderous events.

To come to the foot of Mount Sinai is to face our deeply held apprehensions about faith. We figure this is the place where God means to make us miserable. He will forbid our pleasures and sentence us to a pallid lifetime of wearing light-wash denim and orthopedic brown loafers. As citizens of the twenty-first century, drunk on the wine of autonomy, we view rules like these as straightjacket constrictions. Faith, we assume, will always be the dull gray alternative to multicolored fun.

But this is to misunderstand something significant. The Bible isn't primarily about *rules*; it's about *redemption*. Before any "thou shalt" or "thou shalt not" is pronounced on Mount Sinai, God reminds his people of all the good he's done for them. "I am the Lord your God, who brought you out of the land of Egypt, out of the house of slavery." In other words, the story of God's rescue provides context for the rules. Faith is not primarily about forbiddance but abundance, not primarily about prohibition but invitation. Moses reminds the people that obedience isn't the path of deprivation but the path of life. "You shall walk in all the way that the Lord your God has commanded you, that you may live, and that it may go well with you, and that you may live long in the land that you shall possess." The great paradox of the Bible is that the commands of God make spacious places of our lives. They don't limit our freedom so much as they make true freedom really possible.

As we read these ten words, we get a sense of the kind of people who walk in the ways of God and bear his name in the world. God's people aren't simply devoted to proper rites of worship, although they are committed to worshiping God only. They are also devoted neighbors. They don't observe a stark divide between the holy and the ordinary, the sacred and the secular. They acknowledge that loving God means committing to him the entirety of their Monday through Saturday lives—because he is a jealous God, vying for their undivided allegiance. God's people don't profane what is holy, don't dishonor what is venerable. They honor their parents. They speak the truth. They keep their promises. To hear God's people talk is to notice how they insist more on their responsibilities than their rights.[1] They are free from restless and unrestrained ambition, working hard and practicing rest. They remember who they are because of what God has done.

The Ten Commandments are not God's behavior-management plan for his children. To give special attention to the tenth commandment, the prohibition against coveting, is to see how broadly ambitious God's law is, how absolutely uncompromising it is in its demands. It will never be enough for God to have his people outwardly give and inwardly hoard, outwardly serve and inwardly grouse, outwardly help and inwardly hate. "Thou shalt not covet" aims far deeper than "thou shall not steal." It wills to regulate not simply the act but also the desire. Obedience to the ten words of God is not something performed for audience applause. God aims to transform his people at the deepest levels of intention—before we've yet had the chance to drink our coffee, brush our teeth, and put on something respectable. He aims to produce real virtue in his people, which, as N. T. Wright describes, is what happens when conscious choices to do good and be good become reflexes—or *habit*.[2]

Who can live into these words? God's law can rightly produce despair. But I'm encouraged by a scholar who has noted the "promissory" nature of the law. He has argued that every "shall" and "shall not" of God's commands have less to do with an arm-twisting imperative and more to do with a confident promise.[3] In other words, though it feels impossible to rein in our greed, we *shall* become the kind of people marked by material contentment. Though we can mindlessly defer to habits of deception, we *shall* become the kind of people who consistently bear true witness in the world. And while marriage is hard and vows are more easily broken than kept, we *shall not* be the kind of people who commit adultery.

To read the commands in this way is to see that God is the patient father teaching his children to ride a bike. There will be wobbles and falls and plenty of tears, but God has every confidence in the world that with his help, his children can do it.

Faith shall produce deep, visible, lasting transformation in the lives of God's people.

For Reflection/Discussion

Do you think of God's law as freedom or constraint? Which of the Ten Commandments challenges you most and why?

DAY 7

Read Deuteronomy 6:1–25 (Focus: vv. 4–9)

Key Verse: "These words that I command you today shall be on your heart." (v. 6)

Practice Your Lines

A bony man of nearly seventy, Tom came for dinner at our house, handing me a potted pink orchid as he came through the door and took off his shoes. We learned later, as the candles burned down in the August dark, that ours was the first invitation he had accepted since the death of his wife, to whom he had been married for more than forty years.

After dinner, this former colleague of my husband's cried while speaking of the recent loss of his wife. As an unexpected vulnerability, he also cried when he detailed the trauma of his childhood abuse. "My mother was very, very sick," Tom explained. When he'd met his wife at the university he attended, he'd felt rescued by her. "She saved me," he repeated over and over again, visibly adrift in this new world without her, his cheeks wet with emotion. "I've been so lucky. I've been so incredibly lucky."

We lingered in silence before I decided to breach the rules of polite dinner conversation. "Do you believe in God, Tom?" I had to know if he'd ever considered the possibility that someone else was owed credit for this good life of his.

It isn't just the suffering in life that needs explaining. It's also the delicious sweetness of it. On the one hand, our cultural practice of gratitude is expanding as we're urged to be mindful and give thanks. On the other hand, I wonder where all our vague "thanks" is actually headed. I imagine gratitude lists being cut loose like helium balloons, drifting with the wind, aimless and errant.

Believers in a good and generous God practice gratitude—but not in this vague way of "counting our blessings." Instead, we name our gifts as a way of turning our attention to the Giver. Gratitude, for example, is implied as the only proper response when Israel took possession of the promised land. In Canaan, they would possess a previously inhabited land. They'd populate cities established by other people, reside in homes built by other families, drink water from cisterns dug by other men's hands, eat produce planted by other day laborers.[1] They would put on prosperity like another man's coat, and there could be no crediting their own hard work or skill.

Gratitude is the only proper response to grace.

Take care, Moses commanded, to remember God's grace once the wilderness is behind you. Otherwise, the blessings of the land might become a curse. Because when life is moving placidly along, when the diagnosis is negative and the mortgage is paid, we are easily lulled into habits of self-reliance and self-congratulations. Without clouds in the sky, we are given to forgetting that every ray of sun, every hint of spring is a gift from the Creator and Sustainer God.

The human habit is to forget God. This is why Moses provided a means for remembering, a practice that is still in force today in Jewish synagogues and homes across the globe. It is the twice daily recitation of the Shema: "Hear, O Israel: The Lord our God, the Lord is one. You shall love the Lord your God with all your heart and with all your soul and with all your might."

Rehearsed like lines from a play, the words from Deuteronomy 6:5–9 reminded the people of who God was and what their obligations to him were.[2] God was a God of rescue, and their obedience to him was offered as a response of love. The Shema had none of the stiff formality of classroom learning. It demanded no emotional hype. It was an education woven into the hum of the ordinary and the motion of the everyday: parents talking to children at the house and on the way, from their waking until their sleeping. The Shema was a habit of remembering for God's habitually forgetful people.

The Shema represented words bound upon the hearts of God's people. Moses also commended other physical signage of God's commandments for God's forgetful people. He taught them to bind God's words on their bodies, to post God's words on their doors and city gates. In other words, faith wasn't simply to be nurtured in the inwardness of one's being and in the quietness of the day. It was to be plastered on billboards, made part of the material environment. God meant for faith to be an education of the eye and the body as well as the heart.

I was curious to learn that medieval Jewish philosopher and Torah scholar Maimonides took great confidence in these practices to shore up faith. "The ancient sages said, 'Whoever has *tefillin* [phylacteries] on his head and arm, *tsitsit* [fringes] on his garment, and a *mezuzah* [boxed scroll] on his door may be presumed not to sin for he has many reminders and these are the 'angels' that save him from sinning."[3] But I fear that Maimonides glossed over the reality of the history of Israel and their wandering hearts, a reality that thrums on every page of Deuteronomy. What can really be done for a forgetful people like you and like me, a people whose hearts seem to naturally bend away from God rather than toward him, a people who'd even make God's generosity toward us a cause for rebellion? Will boxes and bindings, even regular recitations of truth, be enough?

To love God with all of our heart, with all of our soul, and with all of our might, we will need more of his help to keep at the habit of remembering.

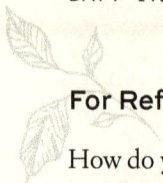

For Reflection/Discussion

How do you experience yourself to be like Israel, a forgetful people in need of a reminder? What concrete thanks can you offer to God today?

DAY 8

Read Deuteronomy 7:1–26 (Focus: vv. 6–11)

Key Verse: "You are a people holy to the Lord *your God."* (v. 6)

His Name Is Jealous

Ryan and I were married just three months after our college graduation. That summer before the wedding, Ryan started working as an actuarial student for a large insurance company outside of Chicago, and I soon began hearing about his cohort—all of them young, none of them married. One particular name kept surfacing in our conversations, and I grew to wonder if *Liz* was nurturing a crush on my fiancé.

That fall, after the wedding, Ryan proposed a double date with Liz and one of his college friends. As the evening wore on, I watched as Liz ignored Scott and fawned over Ryan. Her infatuation was as thick and sweet as Grandma's marmalade, her laughter loud and tinny, rising above the din of the restaurant. Apparently, she found my witty husband even funnier than I did.

This was the last I saw of her.

Such was my first—though certainly not last—brush with jealousy in marriage. It is tempting to think that jealousy signals insecurity in a relationship, that the relationship is inherently fragile if someone is jealous. In a friendship, jealousy certainly can indicate ill health. But it's quite the opposite in marriage. When jealousy flares, the green-eyed response can read like a healthy heartbeat on an EKG. Were there no possessiveness in marriage, there could hardly be love.

My name is Jealous, God told Moses on Mount Sinai,[1] and because I love my people, I won't brook rivals. The covenant that God has made with his people is not an impersonal legal contract. It's a marriage vow, and God is not dispassionate about the terms.[2] He has taken his people for himself, for better or for worse, and he will not mutely suffer their infidelities.

The first of the ten words—"You shall have no other gods before me"—is the command that binds God's people to loyalty to him. Some would say that Deuteronomy 6–8 explains what it means to keep this first commandment. To heed the first word is to keep all of the other nine; to break the first word is to betray the entire list. All sin, in other words, is a form of idolatry. It displaces God from his rightful place of prominence and withholds the love, allegiance, and fear that is due him.

Skeptics would say that this jealous God demands too much obsequiousness and is not to be admired. New Atheist Richard Dawkins has written that the God of the Bible is "arguably the most unpleasant character in all fiction: jealous and proud of it; a petty, unjust, unforgiving control-freak."[3] But Dawkins's accusations can't be easily defended on the basis of what we are discovering in the book of Deuteronomy about this God who loves his unlovely people so gratuitously. Nevertheless, rather than pretend there are no problematic texts in this book, it's important we face the difficulties head-on as we explore a chapter like Deuteronomy 7, which calls for the annihilation of Israel's enemies within the boundaries of Canaan.

First, to examine God's rationale for the destruction of Israel's enemies is to see clearly that while God is jealous, he is not bloodthirsty. He does not choose violence for violence's sake. Rather, he is looking to protect the spiritual faithfulness of his people. He knows their penchant for forgetfulness, that if they fraternize with the Canaanite people, these people's idolatrous influence will prove lethal.[4] Every cultic site, every Canaanite altar must be torn down because Israel is a people who belong to God. Destruction, in this passage, is meant as a means of spiritual preservation.

Further, there's nothing innocuous about the religious practices of these pagan people. The Canaanite people practiced abhorrent rites such as child sacrifice. They consulted the dead, told fortunes, and practiced sorcery. It's not simply that these practices were unhelpful ways of knowing God and entering his presence; they were anathema to true worship. The command to destroy the Canaanites was a decisive judgment against their sin.

In addition, the ban against the Canaanites was never intended as an act of ethnic cleansing. Though we won't read Deuteronomy 13 in our forty days together, we could turn there to see that God commanded infidel Israelite towns to also be destroyed entirely. In Deuteronomy, God commits himself to act swiftly in response to sin, whether he finds the traitors within or outside the boundaries of Israel.

Still, today's reading leaves us with some important questions: Is it okay for God to be jealous of his people? Is it okay for God to judge sin? Dawkins seems to want a God characterized by meekness, whose feathers are never ruffled. He wants a placid, tolerant God who, like a benign middle school principal, feigns ignorance when some shrimp of a kid gets stuffed in a locker.

But this would be a gross miscarriage of justice. Isn't it only *the bully* who wants a tolerant and compassionate god, a god willing to overlook moral faults however small or grievous? If we're the shrimpy seventh grader (or his family), even if we decide on forgiveness, we won't be satisfied by blurry lines of right and wrong. We won't feel consoled when the man with the comb-over tries minimizing the egregiousness of the offense. Justice demands that someone unequivocally pronounce that a line has been crossed, and as a result, a consequence should be levied.

Seen this way, judgment—and jealousy—is part of the goodness of God, and one habit of faith is celebrating it.

Of course, as C. S. Lewis has written, the goodness of God might either be the great danger or the great safety. Who of us can claim that we've only been victim—and never bully? How can we have the full breadth of what we really want from God: both compassion *and* justice, both forgiveness *and* judgment? We will look to answer some of these questions in our reading of the Gospel of John.

For Reflection/Discussion

In what ways are you consoled when you think about God's judgment? In what ways are you terrified?

DAY 9

Read Deuteronomy 8:1–20 (Focus: vv. 1–10)

Key Verse: "You shall remember the whole way that the LORD *your God has led you these forty years in the wilderness."* (v. 2)

Fieldnotes from the Wilderness

We deplaned in the middle of the runway. Heat sizzled from the black tarmac, and we suffocated in its 110 degrees. The next day, riding out of Bamako in the back of a Jeep, we watched a shriveled, brown landscape languishing with the delay of the summer rains. When the road finally ended and we arrived in Macina, the shrunken form of the Niger River was there to greet us. Dead fish littered the dry riverbed.

Our team of five college students had arrived in Mali to work with a Ghanaian doctor for the summer. It was my first real wilderness experience involving mosquito nets (and malaria). Macina was a town located on the northern banks of the Niger River just hours from Timbuktu. Against the backdrop of an endless horizon, it was the kind of desolate place one goes to disappear.

When Moses refers to the "great and terrifying wilderness" that the people of God are leaving behind, it's Macina that I think of. The stark, suffering wilderness behind Israel stands in bold relief to the good, well-watered land of Canaan ahead, supplied by the bounty of its fields and the ore of its hills. Though God has faithfully provided for his people these last forty years, the wilderness has yet been the place of scarcity and hunger. For this reason, it surely seems the place to despise, its memories the ones to blot out.

But Moses warns against this kind of amnesia. Twice he commands them to remember; three times he warns them not to forget. For as bad as the wilderness might have seemed, traveling through it was meant for their good. The wilderness was not simply a way-station. It was the place where the nation was schooled in greater dependence on God.

As the primary example, in the wilderness, God fed his people from his own hand. Six days a week (the seventh day a Sabbath rest), God's people were instructed to leave their tents and gather the mysterious flakes on the ground that had fallen from the sky as they slept, flakes they could grind into flour and knead into bread. Forty years, God fed them like this, literally raining his bread from heaven. He never gave too much, and he never gave too little. But he did give his food as daily bread, and this obliged his people to daily habits of faith. Every morning, they had to renew their confidence in God and his supply.

This God of the manna, who traveled with his people in the great and terrifying wilderness, likens himself to a good and wise father who always knows best. However, his goodness and his wisdom are to be measured not only by the blessings he gives but also by the blessings he withholds. In other words, the scarcity in the wilderness wasn't just a misfortune of the landscape. God lovingly deprived his people for their good. Apart from hunger, how would he teach them that "man does not live by bread alone, but man lives by every word that comes from the mouth of the LORD"?

The wilderness is necessary for the formation of faith. This revelation, of course, does not serve our religious egos. We mean to follow God into our best life now. We want only gifts from him, never lumps of coal. When we stumble into difficulty, we often wonder what wrong turn we took, even how God lost the way. We find ourselves doubting. How can a good God not ensure that every chapter of our lives concludes with "happily ever after"? How can he leave us with illness, fractured relationships, unstable employment, and mounting bills? What could ever be good about hardship?

God never delights in seeing his people suffer, just as parents never delight in seeing their children hurt. Still, good parents know that pain is instructive and sometimes necessary—and God knows that the wilderness has a purging effect. We can't presume to have happiness on our own terms.

The wilderness, as a test of faith, causes us to think of the test that Abraham faced in Genesis 22, when God asked him to take his son, his only son, the son he loved, and sacrifice him to God. Abraham had been told repeatedly that all of God's promises would come through Isaac, which made God's demand seem not just immoral but impossible. It's a story to point to the way faith can upend lives, to suggest how God is in the business of making what seem like crushing demands.

We must put our ear to the ground and hear the drumbeat reminders of Deuteronomy. *Live*, God says. *Live.* I want you to be my people, holy and betrothed to me. I want you to love me above everything else, even your own cramped notions of happiness. As soon as you hand over to me your expectations of what will make your life good, I'll exchange them for promises far more solid and beautiful and lasting.

It reminds me of a story recorded in the Gospels of a rich young man who had initially hoped to become Jesus's disciple. "Sell all that you have and distribute to the poor, and you will have treasure in heaven; and come, follow me," Jesus told him.[1] As it turns out, his sadness was great, for so were his possessions. How could he give to Jesus the keys to the house, to the car, and the password to the bank account, letting him drain it at will? What would he be without all that material scaffolding that propped up his inner sense of stability? It was a sham existence, finding his life in the money under the mattress—but still, it was familiar and one he clung to desperately. If only that man could have believed Jesus's promise that sacrifice wasn't loss but gain.

The God of Deuteronomy is the God of the wilderness—and the God of the lush valleys; the God of manna—and the God of meat; the God of thirst—and the God who brings water from the rock. Truthfully, life is far more precarious than any of us likes to admit. One habit of faith is remembering the lessons of the wilderness in our seasons of prosperity: God can be trusted to lead, even through dry places; hope placed in him is never misplaced hope.

For Reflection/Discussion

Have you ever traveled through a wilderness that, from the other side, you could see was meant for good? What do you make of the idea that we have to surrender to God our expectations for a life immune from suffering?

DAY 10

Read Deuteronomy 9:1–29 (Focus: vv. 13–21)

Key Verse: "Know therefore today that he who goes over before you as a consuming fire is the Lord *your God."* (v. 3)

Signs and Wonders

I make the popcorn, and Eric builds the fire. This has been our self-appointed division of labor since 2011, after our three families moved away from Chicago several years earlier and began gathering nearly every summer for a week in the Adirondack Mountains. It's our habit to end our busy days of swimming, hiking, boating, and pickleball with popcorn and a fire. Sometimes, when the day has been hot, the logs catch fast, spitting, crackling, and roaring to life. We call those fires "ragers." On other nights, when the wood is soggy from the day's previous rain, Eric adds a self-starting log, which lights immediately, the blaze licking upward. But those fires usually die smoldering, smoky deaths. Except for the teenage boys, we don't blame Eric for their fate.

Fire is an image of God throughout the Bible. ("Hellfire and brimstone," some skeptics say.) I won't argue that there isn't fear in today's reading, especially in the retelling of the events of Sinai, where God condescends to meet his people and speak his words to them. There were many ways God could have conducted that audience, but God chose a "rager." The entire mountain was trembling and smoking as God thundered and Moses answered, the fire signaling that God was wholly unapproachable by everyone except

Moses. Were the ordinary people, even the priests, to reach out and touch the base of Mount Sinai, they would be struck dead for their impudence. It was a sensory lesson about the holiness—or wholly other-ness—of God. "Do not fear, for God has come to test you, that the fear of him may be before you, that you may not sin."[1] The heat, the light, the consuming terror of the fire registered, in a physical sense, that it was no trifle, dealing with God.

But Sinai is not the first fire event with which the people of Israel would have been familiar. Perhaps they had heard Moses recount the time, at age eighty, when he'd heard the audible voice of God calling from within a burning bush.[2] A fire raged, but it did not consume. The strangeness of the sight caused Moses to turn aside and lean in with curiosity—although he, too, was warned against coming too close. God spoke that day from the fire, calling Moses by name and commissioning him to lead the nation out of Egypt.

As they left behind the land of slavery, the people of Israel followed God in the form of a pillar of fire. God hadn't equipped the people with coordinates and compasses for their journey. Instead, he traveled with them, showing them the way as a pillar of cloud by day and a pillar of fire by night. That fire was a flaming torch of love, subduing the darkness and striking down fear. It was a light to shepherd them to safety.

There is no one-dimensional way of understanding the fire of God. As Lauren Winner reminds us in *Wearing God*, fire is a paradox: "Fire warms but can blister; fire heats but can consume."[3] In today's reading, we see what the scourge of fire can do. It can lick up the enemies of God, making it possible for Israel to enter the land of Canaan and dispossess its inhabitants. But God's fire can also prove to be an instrument of mercy. Very importantly, as we read in Deuteronomy 9, God's fire devoured the golden calf. The statue representing the false worship of God's people wasn't just pulverized. It was *burned*. And this was to illustrate the kindling power of God's own jealous love. He spared his idolatrous people, refusing to consume them, but he did not spare their idolatries. Those were destroyed. I can't help but wonder if the molten calf was meant as a reminder of the promissory nature of his covenant: "You *shall* have no other gods before me." The fire that consumed the golden calf is kindled by grace.

This chapter is not the rousing *Braveheart* speech we might expect to hear before the people head into battle. Moses didn't hail their courage. Instead, he cataloged all the sites of their wilderness failures: Taberah, where the fire of God fell on the outskirts of the camp, warning a complaining people;[4] Massah, where God brought water from a rock after his people had tested him by wondering, "Is the LORD among us or not?";[5] Kibroth-hattaavah, where the people dug their own "graves of craving" by wishing that meat, not manna, were on the menu;[6] Kadesh Barnea, where they did not trust God's power or promise to give them the land. "You have been rebellious against the LORD from the day that I knew you," Moses concluded in reviewing their travel itinerary. What was clear was that when God brought his people into the land, it would be no credit to their moral virtues.

As we read Deuteronomy with its many rehearsals of God's commands and repeated admonitions to obey, we can't help wondering, in light of Israel's treacherous past, how their future faithfulness will be guaranteed. The nation had been delivered from Egypt by God's "great power and . . . outstretched arm." Still, they continued to prove forgetful and mistrustful. The nation had been accompanied by God in the wilderness, their needs faithfully supplied by him. Still, they persisted in being ungrateful. Even when God had set a mountain on fire with his holy presence, the people wasted no time in abandoning him when Moses lingered too long at the summit. What would cure their fickleness and ensure their loyalty?

We could easily presume that we would have done better in Israel's place, that we would have proven faithful where they had proven faithless. But I know myself too well. In the words of one hymn writer, I am "prone to wander, prone to leave the God I love."[7] I am a spiritual sieve, leaking everything I know to be true about God.

Perhaps the greatest sign and wonder God ever performs is keeping his people faithful to him.

For Reflection/Discussion

What do you think the "fear of God" means in our practical spiritual experience? How do you sense your own need for God's grace?

SHANNON GALVÁN

"From that point I knew:
just like water is wet and birds can fly,
Jesus is real."

Shannon Galván was raised in a family in which evangelical Christianity was considered something American. "As Canadians, we were above that, beyond that, even better than that if I'm being honest." Growing up outside of Toronto, Shannon didn't know people who would have called themselves Christ-followers, although her father was very involved in their local Anglican church. "We would sometimes go with him, but it was very much his thing. If there was going to be brunch or lunch afterward, that was a big motivation [to tag along]."

Shannon and her fraternal twin sister sang in the church choir, but this activity was never considered any more important than any of her other extracurriculars. "It was just like dance class, like playing soccer. And when soccer ramped up for both of us, church, dance, and every other commitment fell by the wayside." If someone had asked Shannon about her personal faith at that time, she would have mentioned her father's church attendance. "That would be it. Sometimes we prayed the Lord's Prayer at bedtime.

Sometimes we prayed as a family at holidays, although not if our extended family was there. We never read the Bible, and no one ever said 'Jesus' out loud. That was too much."

After Shannon left home for college at Bishop's University in Quebec, she describes "three interruptions" in her life, all sent by God. First, as a freshman, she suffered a severe back injury, which forced her to abandon her soccer career. She'd arrived at Bishop's with a scholarship, allowing her to play soccer, but without soccer, "everything stopped. I had these huge questions in life," Shannon admitted. "What were the last ten years for? What am I going to do now?" After back surgery and rehabilitation, Shannon came back to college "totally lost. I tried all of life's vices to make myself feel normal, whatever that meant. But it didn't work at all. I was lonely, and I was confused." After another "shameful evening," Shannon remembered returning to her dorm and asking herself, *Who am I?* That was the moment of the second interruption. "God broke in—this time audibly. He said to me, 'You're mine.'" Although she admitted that it would have been a natural consideration to think she might be hearing voices and losing her mind, Shannon had no doubt this was the voice of God. "I had this hunch: *I think I know who this is. Now I need to investigate.*"

Shannon began attending the campus church at Bishop's (ironically hosted at a local bar) although she admitted that "church" suggested something far more formal and organized than the service she attended. "That Sunday morning, there were four church people in this bar where I worked during the week as a bartender. One had a guitar." Soon, Shannon also added prayer to her spiritual regimen. "*What will it matter?* I thought. I'm either talking to myself in a room or I'm actually talking to God." Additionally, being inclined to research, Shannon began reading the Bible and other Christian writings. She got lost in the dusty religion section of her college library, pulling down volumes from Christian authors whom she recognized: C. S. Lewis, Dietrich Bonhoeffer.

She gravitated, as she told me, to writers whose faith was personal and vibrant. "I already had examples of churchgoers in my life, but I didn't know any Christ-followers." Becoming more familiar with Christian ideas, Shannon would sometimes "try them out" in her college seminar classes, often just to needle the professor and her classmates. "I have a bit of a rebellious streak," she admitted. "But on the other hand, I had such peace. I started to feel like I had direction."

After she graduated from Bishop's, Shannon moved to New York City for a graduate degree in art history and fine art at Pratt Institute. Providentially, the first friend she made at Pratt—Lucy—was a Christian and "a powerful woman of God." Although the two women were in separate programs, they made it their Sunday routine in those early weeks and months to find a church together. "We'd try a church, get lunch, talk, and hang out, and then go our separate ways. It was a nice, consistent touchstone every week." The group of two church shoppers quickly became three when a friend of Lucy's, Alonso, decided to join them. "He was another example of someone who was normal who was also following Jesus." Soon, the three settled at Tim Keller's Redeemer Presbyterian Church, and their weekly routine of church and lunch continued. (Shannon and Alonso were married several years later.)

The third and final "interruption" sent by God was on one of those early Sunday mornings as Shannon trudged to midtown Manhattan from Brooklyn for Redeemer's morning service. "I was thinking, *God, you've got all this city*. That's when he broke in and said, *And I've got you too*." It was the second time that Shannon sensed God speaking to her and it was, in her words, "totally jarring." As she looked down at her feet, her field of vision was completely transformed. "What was just a dirty New York sidewalk became this beautiful concrete thing. The light made it shine. Everything took on this peaceful ombre color. The dust became like strange dew. It was this supernatural moment, and from that point I knew: just like water is wet and birds can fly, Jesus is real."

"That dumb sidewalk is such a moment in my life," Shannon explained. "At nineteen, I had felt like a round peg being jammed into a square hole. My family's politically and socially liberal views never sat comfortably with me. As Christ broke in and introduced me to the world he designed, I found a place where my round peg fit."

"Christianity was like coming home for the first time."

Shannon Galván now calls Charleston, South Carolina, home, where she lives with her wonderful husband, Alonso, and their four children, Lula, Penélope, Vera, and Elías. She has been following Jesus for twenty years.

DAY 11

Read Deuteronomy 10:1–22 (Focus: vv. 1–5)

Key Verse: "Come up to me on the mountain and make an ark of wood." (v. 1)

There's No Place Like Home

Last fall, we began renovating our 1950s Toronto house. Contractors gutted it like a fish and laid forms for a new concrete foundation. Then it rained for nearly three straight weeks. From our rental house just two doors down, I felt like Noah staring from the window of his ark, wondering when the clouds would part.

We've lived in so many houses over the years: houses we've rented, houses we've owned; houses thought to be temporary; houses counted on being permanent. When we moved to Toronto in 2011, we left behind a split level we owned in one of Chicago's western suburbs, which our kids came to call "the brown house." We left behind our grill, our guest bed, and the piano I'd played as a child, planning to come back for it all in several years. We never did. In Toronto, we found a home and decided to stay.

To be human is to long for home. We long to be recognized and received. We're endlessly searching for a welcome that never runs out. Home, as a gift of God, is a dominant theme in the Bible even long before the people of Israel were promised a land. In the beginning, when "God created the heavens and the earth,"[1] he nested like a mother, readying his home for the long-awaited arrival of his beloved children. But this oxygenated planet was not simply a home for humanity; it was also a temple for God.

Creation was a shared home between God and humanity, and in this we discover one of the great paradoxes of the Bible. While God is "God of gods and Lord of lords," he does not remain distant but chooses to draw near, bridging the gap between his loftiness and our lowliness. To him belongs the heaven of heavens. To him also belongs this small nation of people, Israel, who had numbered as few as seventy when God first sent them into Egypt to save them from famine. God's love involves condescension.

In our reading from today, God tells Moses to come up to the mountain, bringing with him an ark of acacia wood. This ark was one of the most important pieces of furniture in the tabernacle, the traveling tent of worship carried throughout Israel's forty years of wilderness wandering. It was also one of the most important pieces of furniture in God's future house—a glorious, gilded temple built by Solomon, third king of Israel. Both the tabernacle and the temple represented God's desire, as old as creation itself, to "dwell with Israel" and to make his home with them.

The ark contained two tablets inscribed by the very finger of God. These tablets were not "Volume 1" and "Volume 2," as is often assumed. Rather, each tablet contained all 171 Hebrew words of the ten words. They were duplicate copies of the "treaty," or covenant, which God had made with Israel. Such was common ancient Near Eastern practice, where the two parties of a treaty each placed a copy of the agreement in the temple of their respective god. The god was then meant to oversee the terms of the treaty and ensure its enforcement.[2]

In Israel's case, there was only one God to enforce the treaty, and it was Yahweh. He was the guarantor of the terms. The ark, then, was representative of his temple, and indeed when the construction of the tabernacle was complete, this small wooden box, overlaid with gold, would stand behind a heavy curtain in a room called

"The Holy of Holies." No one had access to this room except for the high priest, and he, only once a year. God was close—but also cordoned off.

Worship was a mediated affair for the nation of Israel. It involved the work of the few rather than the many. It was not the entire nation who was called up to the summit of Mount Sinai—but Moses. It was not the entire nation who stood before God in the tabernacle to serve and bless him—but the tribe of Levi. In other words, God had a house, but only certain people made it past the parlor. Promixity represented privilege.

To understand the distance God puts between himself and the majority of his people, we must return to the very beginning of the story, in Genesis 1 and 2, when God made a home for Adam and Eve. He threw open the front door and issued a hearty welcome. He played the consummate host, laying a banquet for his children. But there was one house rule, and it was that his children must eat at his table—and his table alone. God's people broke that rule. They refused his generous hospitality and, instead, took up a stranger's offer of forbidden fruit. *They dispensed with the words of God.*

As a result of their sin, Adam and Eve had to leave their garden home and were sentenced to a life of wandering. A *homesick* life. A life where God was more distant than near. But God, being given to mercy and set on relationship, would not let the story end there. He would not leave his people on the outside of the door looking in. He would not suffer long their estrangement from home. In the tabernacle and temple—and as we'll soon learn, in the story of Jesus—God found other ways of drawing near.

A material home, in this world, is often more shadow than reality, more echo than melody. We're all waiting on something better, something more lasting—even on the home we find in God.

One habit of faith is knocking on that door—and expecting it to open wide.

For Reflection/Discussion:

When do you most feel your acute longing for home? What do you make of the idea that home is a gift that God wants to give to his people, even that home is a gift to be found in God himself?

DAY 12

Read Deuteronomy 11:1–32 (Focus: vv. 26–32)

Key Verse: "See, I am setting before you today a blessing and a curse." (v. 26)

Five Words of Faith

I keep a list of names on my phone. They include the names of school parents, neighbors, and recent acquaintances. Joanna is Katie and Bailey's mom; Dan and Jennifer are William's parents. Donna and Peter own Henry, the cocker spaniel who lives around the corner; Ajola and Roan are the Eastern European couple I met at one of Ryan's recent work functions. I've come to rely on this list in middle age, especially when I round the corner with our dog and ask myself, yet again, if my neighbor several doors down is named Randall or Russell.

Growing up, I unsympathetically lamented my own mother's penchant for forgetting. It's why I've tried, albeit imperfectly, to remember my own children's lives—or at least to write a few things down. In their early years, I cataloged the memories in birthday photo albums I gave every year as gifts. After a recent move, the albums were unpacked by one of my eleven-year-old twins, and he spent an evening pouring over them, laughing aloud. "I walked at *eighteen* months," he corrected. (The day before, I'd told him fifteen.)

Memory is an important impulse of Deuteronomy. Though the book strains its neck toward the future as Moses readies the people to possess the promised land, and though it's also a book fixated on "now" and the present-tense invitations of faith, we are also sure to notice how Deuteronomy cranes its neck toward the past. *Remember*, Moses keeps insisting, like it's the chorus of a contemporary worship song on endless repeat. However, if the stories we've read up to this point were recorded as photographs in an album, those images would not look like the filtered images we see on Instagram. Instead, Israel is cast in a harsh, unforgiving light.

Making a narrative tour through their failures, Moses remembers their quick plunge into idolatry on Mount Sinai when they made a golden calf and bowed down to it. Moses recounts episodes of complaint and, in greater detail, their failure to obey God at Kadesh Barnea forty years earlier. History has proven that Israel has been a forgetful, unfaithful people.

But Moses not only remembers Israel's shortcomings in the long-winded retrospective that is Deuteronomy. He also takes stock of God's steadfast love and faithfulness. In one of the longest sentences in the entire Hebrew Bible, from verses 2 through 6, Moses puts God's power on display, remembering how he delivered Israel at the Red Sea by drowning the pursuing Egyptian army; how he miraculously judged the traitors within the camp, opening the earth to swallow them whole. These severe judgments were referred to as a "lesson" in the Tanakh translation of the Hebrew Bible: "Take thought this day that it was not your children, who neither experienced nor witnessed the *lesson* of the LORD your God" (v. 2, emphasis added).[1] These events in Israel's history were never just dates for a time line. They invited Israel to know who God is by virtue of seeing what God *does*. Their seeing was a means of knowing, their knowing a means of believing. As a habit of faith, memory promised to shore up their confidence for the road ahead.

Five verbs are repeated throughout the book of Deuteronomy (and later in the book of John, making for many natural parallels between these two books). They are *see*, *know*, *love*, *obey*, *live*.

These five words tell us much about the habits of faith. They remind us that faith isn't blind but asks us to consider the evidence: *see*. They teach us that faith, though not infallible certainty about everything, is yet confident understanding based on God's concrete self-revelation: *know*. They insist that faith is not impersonal but intimate, as much a matter of the heart as the mind: *love*. They warn against faith that's nominal and shallow, more lip service than life practice: *obey*.

In the Pentateuch, the command to "love God" is a command unique to Deuteronomy. Although it might seem to be the most sentimental of the five words, because love is most often paired with "obey," we learn in this book what love for God really looks like. It has hands and feet. It bears ethical commitments. In fact, the love of God demands obedience to the particular laws in chapters 12–26, laws that we won't examine in depth. These laws govern every aspect of the life of the nation: domestic, civic, religious, social, economic. In the book of Deuteronomy, we don't *feel* faith so much as we *do* faith. Faith is a habit of being in the world that is intensely practical and public.

Four of these five verbs take God as their object. We see God, know God, love God, obey God. He is the sun, and we are the planets orbiting around him.

However, one of the five words does not have God as its object. It's the verb *live*, and its subject is humanity. We are invited to live, to flourish, and to thrive. This word suggests that faith is not the masochist affair we make of it, that God is not the sadist we believe him to be. Though the word *live* appears explicitly in other places in Deuteronomy, here in chapter 11, it's simply alluded to as Moses calls out the choice before the nation of Israel as they stand in the plains of Moab. Here the road forks: Will they choose a blessing, or will they choose a curse?

Live. This word represents the shocking self-interest of faith, and any parent will be familiar with this kind of plea. We teach our children to nurture habits that will keep them safe and healthy, that will make their lives better, not worse. Brush your teeth. Hold my hand when you cross the street. Look both ways. Eat your vegetables. We could tell our children to obey these rules because we're the parent and we've said so. (Sometimes, this is exactly what needs to be said.) Still, a far more persuasive strategy is to remind them of the good they secure for themselves when they choose to obey. *Live.*

Before I was a Christian, I used to believe that faith wasn't simply a narrow road but a cold, damp, and miserable one. I thought God relished every opportunity to test the mettle of my faith; I thought he worked to make its everyday experience pinch, if even just a little. But this is not the picture of the God of Deuteronomy, the God who pleads for his children to choose blessing and *live*.

For Reflection/Discussion

To which of these five words of faith do you react the most? To what degree have you considered that the life of faith is the environment of true living and the means of true human flourishing?

DAY 13

Read Deuteronomy 26:1–19 (Focus: vv. 16–19)

Key Verse: "This day the Lord *your God commands you to do these statues and rules."* (*v. 16*)

Worrying for God's Reputation

"Will you still go to church when you're grown up?" One of Colin's friends asks this as I drive the two boys to soccer practice. My youngest son, Colin, looks pained, as if the answer isn't obvious. "Yeeeesssss," he answers emphatically, his voice stretching, then snapping like a rubber band.

Church was a sore subject with Colin's soccer team. In the fall, we'd registered our son for a slightly more serious league, at least more serious than our neighborhood league. In the winter, when he asked to continue playing in this two-practice, one-game-a-week league, we noted that the games were now slated for Sundays, not Saturdays.

"We don't do activities on Sundays," we reminded Colin, who had an easy and immediate solution to offer. "But church is only from 9:30 until 10:45!" It seemed that he favored one consecrated hour rather than an entire holy day.

"Observe the Sabbath day, to keep it holy." This was the fourth of the ten words given to Israel on Mount Sinai. It was a strict boundary around work and also an invitation to rest. As a Christian family who practices Sabbath, we don't count ourselves bound to this commandment in the same way that Israel was. Rather, we keep it because it's a life-giving habit in a 24/7 world. It's a pause in the hurry and the hustle of a week, a way to mitigate our self-destructive busyness.

Unlike Israel, we do not live in a theocracy governed by God.[1] This is one reason I've chosen to omit from our reading schedule chapters 12–25, which catalog the commands that governed Israel's national life. Still, it seems vital to summarize some of what we've skipped in these chapters. Most importantly, it's worth noting that these laws were not rules to earn God's favor. Instead, they served to remind the people of their identity.

"You are a holy people," God reminds Israel many times throughout the book of Deuteronomy. This holiness was as much about their relationship to the surrounding nations as it was about their moral choices. The people of Israel were called to *otherness.* They were forbidden to assimilate. They were to eat differently, work differently, worship differently, mourn differently. In fact, when there was no apparent moral rationale for some of the laws, one reason always remained outstanding. God had said: my people must recognizably be mine. They must be different, even alien.

Certainly not all the laws in Deuteronomy are as seemingly arbitrary as forbidding Israel from eating shellfish, wearing two kinds of fabric, and boiling a young goat in its mother's milk. Even to our contemporary ears, tuned to the high frequency of justice, we see the remarkably progressive nature of Israel's covenant law. Because God was just, he forbade predatory lending practices and the exploitation of hired workers. He instituted rules that protected the immigrant, the widow, and the orphan. He commanded asylum for runaway slaves coming from neighboring nations. Justice, according to God, involved actively seeking a neighbor's good, even chasing after his wandering ox if he should be caught sauntering by your open kitchen window.[2]

But not every law in Deuteronomy accommodates our contemporary standards of rightness. There are irreducible difficulties in some of the laws. There was no prohibition against slavery. Capital punishment was the sentence of judgment meted out for false prophets, blasphemers, entire apostate villages, rebellious children, adulterers—even rape victims who were accused of failing to cry for help. Foreign female captives, taken like plunder in war, were not afforded a voice when Israelite men slavishly made them wives.

When I impose my twenty-first century sensibilities on this ancient text, I can worry for God's reputation, perhaps even the primitiveness of biblical faith. But maybe an important place for me to begin is admitting the subjectivity of my response. I am a white, educated woman living in North America. Can I defend that the judgments I render about right and wrong are entirely objective? I don't, for example, share some of my Korean friends' conviction about paying their aging parents a monthly stipend as a way of repaying their gratitude.

We do well to remember that the Bible is an ancient, enculturated text. It comes to us from a certain time, a certain place. This is not to moderate the claim that the Bible is a God-breathed book, speaking infallible truth, but it is to underline some tensions we readers confront when we read God's book. There is the paradox of its being wholly divine—and also wholly human. There is the paradox of its being "living and active"—and also time-bound. There is the paradox of its being clear—and also requiring interpretation.

My sixteen-year-old son is reading the Bible and grappling with some of these paradoxes. I see how he wants a book that stands outside of time, a book that resolves every question and tolerates no ambiguity. He wants the Bible to be exhaustive, to be read like an instruction manual. But as I've wondered aloud with him, I'm not sure that faith could be formed by such a book. To read such a book would make something formulaic of faith, something robotic of believers. It would require no ultimate dependence on God.

I told my son that one of the best ways of reading these ancient laws is to ask, How did they differ from other ancient law codes?[3] What do those differences tell us about the kind of people God wanted Israel to be? And ultimately, what do these laws tell us about the lawgiver, God himself? If these rules bear out "his ways," then what path does God travel? I shared with him how I was helped by Old Testament scholar Mary Willson, who taught that these laws were never meant to establish a perfect, sinless society—a new garden of Eden. Instead, God gave his people a code by which they could restrain their sinful, selfish impulses.[4] The law always anticipated that God had something better to give.

As I practice the Sabbath today, I think of it less as a fixed commandment and more as a principle of wisdom, restraining my greed and tireless ambition. To refrain from working one day of seven, even to refrain from the call to chauffeur my children to and from their myriad activities, invites me into the bodily trust that the world will keep spinning when I choose to pause. Moreover, it points me to the Giver—and gift—of an even greater rest.

As always proves true, I find greater freedom, not less, in submitting myself to a law higher than my own desires.

For Reflection/Discussion

How is your confidence in the Bible impacted by what you've learned about some of its laws? What would be easier—and also limiting—if the Bible were an unabridged instruction manual of faith?

DAY 14

Read Deuteronomy 27:1–26 (Focus: vv. 1–8)

Key Verse: "Keep the whole commandment that I command you today." (v. 1)

The Question of Appetite

Food is love. At least that's how I understood it growing up. It was nothing to count on eggs for breakfast every day of the week, nothing to expect a three-layered German chocolate cake every year on my birthday, the shredded coconut frosting pooling at its base because Mom had rushed to frost it.

I have strived to imitate my mother in her dogged commitment to both food and love. When we returned from our honeymoon more than twenty years ago, I made a towering chocolate cake and greeted Ryan with it his first day home from the office. Just this morning, after the world had turned white in the night, I warmed milk on the stove until a thin skin formed on its surface, then added hearty spoonfuls of Dutch cocoa and agave nectar. I buttered slices of fresh sourdough bread and removed the centers to fry eggs in the holes. With food, I try persuading my family that there's one warm corner of the world they can count on.

I can't help noticing the eating that the Israelites are doing in chapter 27. (A food ceremony is also at the center of chapter 26.) First, Israel must take large steles and inscribe them with the law of God.[1] This symbolizes how permanent and solid God's words are intended to be. Perhaps wind and weather will erode the surface of these stones, but we get the sense that God's words will resist decay. Then, the people of God will take other stones and make an altar of offering to God. They will burn the flesh of animals and roast the yield of the land. They will eat, rejoicing before the Lord their God.

The mention of this "table" is so slight as to be nearly inconspicuous, but it reminds me just how much of Israel's religious life circled around food, how feasting is an important habit of faith. To be sure, God commanded times of obligatory fasting, but those occasions of deprivation were more exception than rule. What was more common for God's people was the gathering of families around food, telling stories of what God had done for them. We often imagine spiritual commitment to be a sallow affair, as if the only way to serve God is on an empty stomach. But in ancient Israel, the most sacred moments of the year smelled like roasted lamb and freshly baked loaves.

If worship was an invitation to indulge certain appetites, it was also an invitation to restrain others. In this chorus of curses, which the Levites are commanded to call out and to which the people are to respond "Amen!" we see that God arbitrates the sexual drives of his people. Of course, there's more here than sexual rules, and the commands outlined in chapter 27 can be correlated to each of the ten words. Further, there is nothing particularly offensive in the list of sexual prohibitions, which forbids sex with animals and sex with family members. Yet on the other hand, we don't have to look far in the Bible to see other sexual prohibitions that offend in our culture of "love is love." In both the Old and New Testaments, God reveals he intends for human beings to enjoy sex in the context of heterosexual, monogamous marriage.

It's worth noting that the Bible never affirms the ethic of individual freedom as the sole arbiter of right and wrong. We aren't free to do whatever feels good, even if it seems to be harming no one. One important point of Deuteronomy is the locus of spiritual authority. *These are the words.* We don't look primarily inward for truth, letting feelings and desires govern our moral choices. Rather, we look upward, believing that God has invested his words with ultimate authority. In fact, the Bible spins its own tale of tragedy when people choose to do what is right in their own eyes.[2]

Submitting our sex lives to God might be one of the hardest things we do in the life of faith. But this predicament is not new to modern life. No, in the early church, it was the sexual choices of Christians that set them apart from their pagan neighbors. To bear witness to the living Christ, they didn't canvas their neighborhoods with hokey religious tracts, rally protests, or start a homeschooling co-op. Instead, as one example of their ethical "otherness," they practiced *chastity.* They kept sex in marriage; they kept sex for marriage.

As I write in these pages, I want to do as Jesus did, which is to be absolutely unapologetic about the nature of faith's demands. God does not mean to leave us unchanged. In the New Testament, Jesus likened the life of faith to building a tower. If someone wanted to engage in an expensive and time-consuming project, they needed to have a realistic sense of the price tag. And faith, with its every lavish benefit, its every real reward, does beg us to count a cost. In fact, at certain points in Jesus's ministry, when he said difficult things, the crowds left in droves. In the wake of their departure, Jesus asked his disciples: "Do you want to go away as well?"[3] He understood that his words didn't always console; they often chafed.

Moses stands before Israel with the elders of the people, insisting they obey the "whole commandment." In one sense, it's strange to describe the law of God in the singular. After all, we've just skipped fourteen chapters of rules! In another sense, this idea—that the word of God is not plural—is an important one.

There is an elegant simplicity to the life of faith, and God calls us to give our whole selves to him.

For Reflection/Discussion

When are you tempted to diminish certain commandments in favor of others? Which areas of your life would you prefer *not* to be God's business?

DAY 15

Read Deuteronomy 28:1–68 (Focus: vv. 58–68)

Key Verses: "If you faithfully obey the voice of the Lord *your God, . . . all these blessings shall come upon you and overtake you."* (*vv.* 1–2)

No Mercenary Affair

When our oldest son, Nathan, was in the seventh grade, he memorized all fourteen stanzas of Henry Wadsworth Longfellow's "Paul Revere's Ride" for a school poetry slam. On the afternoon of the competition, Nathan came home dejected. "I didn't win," he said. "What? Who did?" We couldn't imagine someone outperforming Nathan's flawless recitation of Longfellow's 143 lines, his voice driving like the hooves of Revere's horse. "Elizabeth," he admitted, his older sister groaning. Elizabeth had the reputation of a glossy-braids teacher's pet.

Nathan's surprise upset has become mythology in our family, a story to tell and retell. I could still sound sore about the travesty of Nathan's upset (Do I still sound sore?) except for what the players on the seventh-grade girls' basketball team told Nathan, their assistant coach, a couple of weeks ago. It was his recitation, not Elizabeth's, that had been held up as an example by his former teacher when she announced this year's slam.

Poetry is made for remembering, especially the kind with the pulsing rhythm and rhyme of Longfellow's "Paul Revere's Ride." What we can't appreciate, in our reading today, are the similar poetic elements of Deuteronomy 28. In the Hebrew, this long list of blessings and curses, a familiar genre in the ancient Near East, sings with repetition and alliteration. Because it reads like poetry, it is sticky. It gets caught in the gossamer of unconscious thought. It's a list meant for oral performance.

As we learned in Deuteronomy 27, on the day of crossing the Jordan into the promised land, Israel is to organize itself by tribe. On Mount Gerizim, the tribes of Simeon, Levi, Judah, Issachar, Joseph, and Benjamin will call out the blessings of God meant as reward for the people's obedience: "Blessed be your basket and your kneading bowl." On Mount Ebal, the tribes of Reuben, Gad, Asher, Zebulun, Dan, and Naphtali will assemble to call out the curses for the nation, should they choose not to be "careful to do all the words of this law that are written in this book." The blessings and the curses touch every aspect of common life. (Given that four times more space is dedicated to the curses, it is easy to surmise what the future holds for God's people.)

Important questions emerge out of this public ceremony of blessings and curses. We could wonder if what's being illustrated here is a principle akin to karma, this axiom in Buddhism and Hinduism that good people inherit good things and bad people inherit evil things. As a system, it draws straight lines between good behavior and reward, between bad behavior and punishment. Karma helps people understand their standings before God, manage his good opinion, even stave off the suffering of cancer and unemployment, infertility and bankruptcy. It's a call to behave.

Truthfully, there are lots of "Christian" books, podcasts, and Cheshire-grinned preachers that preach exactly this. They peddle a version of faith in God that is more a faith in prosperity. You go to church, you give money away, you abandon your bad habit of swearing. Then you picture yourself in a pimped-out sports car, zipping through the city streets with the wind in your (never graying, never balding) hair. Why have the curse when you can have the blessing?

But such distortion proves why we must read the Bible in its entirety. Verses are not to be extracted like teeth. In the book of Job, we see the suffering of a righteous man, not an evil one. If anyone seemed deserving of the blessings, it was Job. But for reasons not entirely clear, God allows Job to enter days that are black and bleak, to suffer the loss of his children, his property, his good health. Job is a man stripped naked, and God refuses to answer Job's howling why.

Job's friends assume that Job's sin is the reason for his suffering. They draw their own crude lines between good behavior and reward, between bad behavior and punishment. But it turns out that they're grossly wrong—so wrong that at the end of the story, when Job's suffering is finally ended and his fortunes restored, God commands Job to intercede for his foolish friends.

On Mount Ebal, curses for disobeying God are shouted into the wind; on Mount Gerizim, blessings for obeying him. If Job had been standing there, I wonder how he would have made sense of his burning skin covered in boils, how he would have explained the cruel loss of his ten children—happy and healthy one day, buried the next. Job came to learn, as all believers must, that while there is blessing to be found in faith, faith in God is no guarantee of material prosperity and lasting good health.

The broad witness of Scripture never teaches that faith immunizes us from pain. However, it does assure us of this: there is blessing, both temporal and eternal, for loving and obeying God. Blessing is inherent to the life of faith. For one, to obey God, the Creator of all things, and to live by his words is to follow the moral grain of the universe and be spared the horror of sin.[1] God doesn't command obedience simply because it pleases him. He commands it because it's the path of our greatest flourishing. Similarly, God doesn't forbid sin simply because it displeases him; he forbids it because sin always proves to be the rot and ruin of our lives.

The twentieth-century British author C. S. Lewis wrote that faith is not the mercenary affair we sometimes make of it. We do not need to be ashamed of wanting the blessing rather than the curse. We are self-preserving creatures, and this is not a moral flaw, something to be overcome by severe asceticism and self-flagellation. "If there lurks in most modern minds the notion that to desire our own good and earnestly to hope for the enjoyment of it is a bad thing, I submit that this notion has crept in from Kant and the Stoics and is no part of the Christian faith."[2] In other words, though we can't presume upon the future, what God will and won't do, what he will and won't give, we have every right to hunger for blessing. And faith is a means of blessing.

"Blessed be your basket and your kneading bowl."

For Reflection/Discussion

In your own life, have you seen the correlation between blessing and obedience, curse and disobedience? In seasons of difficulty, have you ever, like Job, wondered if you didn't deserve better from God?

KEVIN FEIYU LI

"I planned a lot of things in my life.
Being a Christian was never one of them."

Growing up in Communist China, Kevin was an atheist. His exposure to Christianity was scant—"maybe one paragraph in an academic book over an entire year's [course of study]." Culturally, he was influenced by Confucian, Taoist, and Buddhist ideas, although he never arrived at any kind of "consistent worldview or satisfying answer to the meaning of life." Like most native-born Chinese, he believed that "human beings are fundamentally good, teachable, improvable, and perfectible through personal endeavor and self-cultivation." If there was a god, it was oneself.

Kevin came to Canada to study undergraduate physics at Western University, and his spiritual curiosities were ignited by two books: the first, physicist Erwin Schroedinger's *What Is Life?*, which tackled both material and metaphysical questions; the second, philosopher Baruch Spinoza's *Ethics*. Kevin began to interrogate the wishful thinking of his childhood, which seemed to him almost a system of faith. He recognized that it lacked coherence and a grounding in objective reality. At the same time, he chafed at adopting any kind of belief system beyond himself, which might run counter to his most fundamental desires. "These questions started a battle in me. I was trying to resolve the conflicts between desire and belief. I wanted things that were beneficial to myself."

At Western, Kevin's exposure to Christians was still very limited. After a breakup with a long-term girlfriend, he was walking dejectedly across campus when several Christians approached him, inviting him to their student fellowship. "It was so foreign to me," Kevin admitted, "and I thought they were conspiring [to convert me]." He politely refused their invitation. Several weeks later, he was approached by a different group of people—this time, Mormons. They invited him to church, and almost to his own surprise, he agreed. "It was the first time I actually tried to be at peace with myself and to seek for answers." Becoming preoccupied with his studies, Kevin attended the Mormon church only two or three times before quitting. "It planted a seed for looking into religion as a whole."

In 2016, Kevin came to Toronto to begin his graduate studies in industrial engineering. After responding to an ad on Facebook, he leased an apartment with two other graduate students, one of whom had been raised by a Christian mother. At the time, Jeff claimed no personal commitment to Jesus, although Kevin recounted when all of that changed for Jeff. He and Kevin had been in a campus building for another student meeting when they noticed a Christian group in the classroom right beside them. Jeff wanted to infiltrate the meeting. "It was a bit silly. He had the idea that maybe he could convince people out of Christianity."

Jeff attended the Christians' group meeting and talked to Kevin about it later that night in their apartment. Apparently, Jeff had been the one convinced. Jeff began reading his Bible and attending these student ministry meetings regularly. At first, Kevin was miffed with his roommate's new faith: "Why did you switch sides?" However, when he began going to these meetings with Jeff, Kevin couldn't help but notice the genuine love and hospitality of those who attended. It became a safe place to ask questions and observe the lives of Christ-followers.

"For the next two years, I engaged in constant dialogue with myself and debate with my roommate, Jeff. Every day, we debated the existence of God; other religions; the foundation of truth, knowledge, morality; as well as the life, death, and resurrection of Jesus; and the consistent revelation of Scripture." Kevin laughed to admit, "I would get destroyed." At first, the idea of a personal God was a foreign, even a frightening concept. Kevin also struggled to reconcile belief in supernatural events (e.g., the resurrection of Jesus) and supernatural beings (e.g., angels and demons). "That was a real stumbling block in coming to Christ. I wanted God to prove himself to me."

Little by little, however, Kevin's secular worldview was shattered, and he could no longer deny the truth of Christianity, even if he also feared what he perceived to be faith's onerous demands. "I thought that being a Christian meant meeting a checklist: praying frequently, reading the Bible daily, going to [Christian meetings] a lot. That was a burden to me, too big a commitment." Still, those fears eroded as he began attending church in Toronto, where he started to conceive that Christian faith was less about "responsibilities" and more about "a relationship with our heavenly Father."

But while Kevin became logically convinced that Christianity was the only consistent worldview, while he began to understand Christianity's invitation to friendship with God, he still did not leap to becoming a Christian. "I didn't want to have any boundaries in my life. I wanted freedom—freedom to pursue all my desires." He remembered another late-night conversation with Jeff and another Christian friend, Gabe, where he exploded in frustration. "You know what? I am annoyed. Let's stop the Christianity discussion. I want to do whatever I want, even if it means going to hell." Gabe had been shocked and asked simply if they could pray together. "[It was] a prayer that I would never forget. Gabe said in a trembling voice, 'God, please draw Kevin closer to you.' Afterward, I laughed and added, 'Yeah, if you're out there.'"

A month later, Kevin was casually eating lunch with Jeff, who showed him an already familiar passage of Scripture from one of the apostle Paul's letters, 1 Corinthians 13. Jeff read aloud about the qualities of love—that it's patient and kind, that it does not envy or boast, that it is not proud, self-seeking, or easily angered. That it always protects, always trusts, always hopes, always perseveres; that love never fails. "Those words produced in me overwhelming emotions—emotions that I had never experienced before." Five minutes later, Kevin confessed that he was a sinner, that Jesus Christ had died for his sins, and that Jesus was Lord of his life. "I planned a lot of things in my life. Being a Christian was never one of them. But by God's grace and his plan, I became a child of God on that day."

Kevin Feiyu Li is a graduate student in industrial engineering at the University of Toronto. He attends Grace Toronto Church.

DAY 16

Read Deuteronomy 29:1–29 (Focus: vv. 18–28)

Key Verse: "To this day the Lord *has not given you a heart to understand or eyes to see or ears to hear."* (v. 4)

No Cherry-Cheeked Santa Claus

Our friends Sandy and Thomas married later in life. They wanted to have children and didn't wait long after their wedding day to start trying for a family. But the years bore barrenness, then ectopic pregnancies, then the loss of one of Sandy's ovaries. Eventually, they buried their dream of having biological children and began nurturing the hope of international adoption. Several years later, two children came to them from across the ocean.

When they came home with their second child, friends and family gathered to greet them at the airport, brandishing signs and balloons. We buzzed with excitement to see them emerge (bedraggled) from the terminal. When I finally had my turn to welcome this miracle, I couldn't help but scream spontaneously with joy. Their newly adopted daughter began to wail.

When I come to Deuteronomy 29, it's adoption that I think of. Adoption requires a process by which belonging is formalized, and this is the ceremony pictured in our reading today. The noisy crowd of a nation has gathered for the event, and as I imagine it, babies are wailing and mothers are swaying to shush them. Young children are perched on the strong shoulders of their fathers. The gray-haired are wishing for a place to sit down.

It's a different scene from forty years earlier, when the nation had gathered at the smoking base of Mount Sinai. There is no fire, no smoke, no threatening sky. Instead, Moses seizes this moment as yet another occasion to remind the nation of all the good that God has done for them: rescue from slavery, provision in the wilderness, recent defeat of the kingdoms of Heshbon and Sihon. These stories are now part of their national history, and they beg to be told and retold.

(We live by the stories we tell.)

But as much as the nation has *seen* of God these last forty years, they've also proven blind. Moses says that they had eyes but didn't see, ears but didn't hear. They had facts—but they didn't have faith. They lacked "a heart to understand." In other words, if faith is to penetrate the hard clay of the human heart, if it is to take deep root, we must be convinced at levels deeper than the intellect. Faith is not the same thing as geometric proof.

One truth, apprehended only by faith, is that we are sinners in need of a Savior. I know how stodgy and churchy *sin* can sound to people. Sin seems like a word borrowed from sweaty preachers and slick televangelists: guilt in exchange for your donation. But in his unfinished apology for the Christian faith, *Pensées*, Blaise Pascal clung to the idea that the preaching of sin is a healing rather than a harm. "The great barrier to happiness," Pascal wrote, "is our refusal to accept that we are at fault."[1] Sin, in other words, is an invitation to mend things by accepting responsibility. It is to lay down the practice of making excuses for ourselves and to face, clear-eyed, our habit of breaking things willfully. Faith is an agreement of complicity.

The vivid picture of verse 18 is of an unrepentant sinner who doesn't consider the loyalty and obedience he owes to God. Translated in the Tanakh, it reads: "He may fancy himself immune, thinking, 'I shall be safe, though I follow my own willful heart.'"[2] This person does not submit to the binding authority of God's words, much like a wild horse does not submit to the bridle or bit. It's not that he hasn't heard the words of God; it's that he has dismissed them, emptying them of their threat.

Perhaps this person is someone who can't imagine that a good God would levy curses on the people he loves, especially the well-intentioned ones. Maybe his god is a cherry-cheeked Santa Claus whose only job is to deliver toys to the children. But this isn't the God of the Bible, a God who is full of goodness and steadfast mercy, keeping every promise he makes—no matter how terrible. At Sodom and Gomorrah, God even made good on his promise to rain down judgment on these sinful cities of the plain.[3]

To revisit that terrible story of God's severe judgment is to remember the role of Abraham, who had hoped to spare God the necessity of judging Sodom. He pled with God to do justly. He asked him to refuse to punish the righteous alongside the wicked. He bargained with God for the salvation of the city, and as it turns out, none of this took any real convincing. God agreed to spare Sodom for the sake of ten righteous people.

But tragically, even this small remnant could not be found. Sodom was a city whose every resident, save Lot, his wife, and his two daughters, thought themselves safe in their sin.[4] In fact, when Lot, Abraham's nephew and resident of Sodom, went to warn his sons-in-law of God's pending judgment, they laughed.[5] To remember the curses of Deuteronomy against the backdrop of Sodom is to be duly warned that God's words are not to be trifled with.

There's a sobriety, even a fear, involved in faith. Nevertheless, God's mercy echoes even in the midst of judgment. In this chapter, we see that the curse of sin seems to fall more on the land than on the people. It's the land that's afflicted, the land that is sick, the land against which "the anger of the Lord [is] kindled." This brings to mind the very first curses of the Bible in Genesis 3 when Adam and Eve ate the forbidden fruit. There too God cursed the land—sparing, in one sense, the immediate judgment of his people.[6] Of course it's not possible to separate the flourishing of the land with the flourishing of its inhabitants, but it could suggest that in administrating his justice, God patiently gives sinners an opportunity to repent.

The God of the Bible is as committed to mercy as he is to justice, to justice as he is to mercy. Faith recognizes both aspects of God's character.

For Reflection/Discussion

How easily do you practice the habit of confessing your sin? What freedom comes in admitting the truth about yourself, even that you're morally flawed and in need of God's forgiveness?

DAY 17

Read Deuteronomy 30:1–20 (Focus: vv. 1–6)

Key Verse: "And the LORD your God will circumcise your heart and the heart of your offspring, so that you will love the LORD your God with all your heart and with all your soul, that you may live." (v. 6)

Heart Surgery

I am a homebody. Before COVID-19, this almost felt like a moral failing. Though it's never been easier to plan a travel itinerary, book a flight, or choose a restaurant in an unfamiliar city, I usually prefer staying put. Even when I do travel, I generally forgo the research and the obligatory social media posts.

My trip to Berlin a couple of years ago could have been vastly improved with a little bit of historical review. Having grown up in the eighties, I retained a vague understanding of the Cold War, but I'd not learned, or at least not remembered, an important speech that John F. Kennedy delivered in West Berlin. Standing before 120,000 West Berliners on June 26, 1963, Kennedy roused the crowd with a refrain of civic solidarity: "Ich bin ein Berliner." These four words, which Kennedy had scribbled on his speech just minutes before taking the stage, were repeated again and again to the roars of the crowd. "I am a Berliner!"

Deuteronomy captures rhetorically memorable moments like that one. In each of Moses's three speeches delivered in the plains of Moab, he relies upon repeatable turns of phrase that replay throughout the book and, if successful, in the minds of God's people. In the first speech, he calls upon Israel to "listen to the statutes and the rules that I am teaching you, and do them, that you may live."[1] In the second speech, he insists that "the LORD commanded us to do all these statutes, to fear the LORD our God, for our good always, that he might preserve us alive, as we are this day."[2] In the third speech, which concludes our reading today, he closes with this: "Therefore choose life, that you and your offspring may live, loving the LORD your God, obeying his voice and holding fast to him, for he is your life and length of days." What Israel must understand is that when they choose to obey God, they will preserve and prosper their lives. They will have blessing, not curse. They will *live*.

As we've seen elsewhere in the book, Moses bends time when addressing God's people. At first, he speaks to them as if they are a generation past: not the children but the fathers who'd been delivered from Egypt. Then he speaks to them as if they are a generation future: not the children of that Exodus generation but their grandchildren. In the plains of Moab, all are invited into a present-tense faith—with its habits of seeing and knowing, its habits of living and loving and obeying.

One particular mystery emerges from our reading today, something to puzzle us as we read carefully. On the one hand, Moses insists there's no inherent difficulty in apprehending God's word. It's not distant but near, not hidden but revealed, not mysterious but plain, not difficult but easy. "It is in your mouth and in your heart, so that you can do it." But given what we've learned of Israel's story, this seems like an exaggerated confidence. What has appeared most plain in Deuteronomy has been Israel's incapacity for obeying God's words. In fact, at the beginning of chapter 30, Moses reveals that God's people will eventually fail to keep the covenant and, as a result, be scattered from the land. If the covenant is so easy to keep, why does Israel seem poised to make a wreck of it?

Verse 6 answers some of our curiosities. It reveals how God intends to heal the spiritual deformity of his people—this inward bent away from him rather than toward him. He will circumcise their hearts. For those lacking familiarity with the story of Abraham, we might wonder about God's verb of choice. *Circumcise* the heart? But this hearkens back to Genesis 17, when the octogenarian is called by God to become the father of nations. At the bodily point of promise, God inscribes belonging. He tells Abraham to have himself and all the men in his household circumcised, making the removal of the foreskin a visible symbol of a new identity.

As the Bible bears out in its story from Genesis to Revelation, we can't really become God's people by rites performed upon the body. In order to heal the problem of sin, we must submit to a surgery of the heart, where God removes the cancer of our stubbornness. If we are to obey his commands willingly, he must give us new desires beyond those that feel most instinctive to us, even those that feel most right. As Saint Augustine, church father of the fourth century, said in so many words, God must reorder our disordered loves, making it possible for us to love him and love our neighbors as ourselves. This is a healing work that he will perform by his own grace, proving our need for something greater than willpower, something more enduring than New Year's resolutions. Faith in the God who heals by his grace is like the faith of a patient before he's wheeled into the operating room. He knows that the operation will succeed because of the surgeon's skill, not his own competence or cooperation as patient.

As we near the end of the book of Deuteronomy and the foregone conclusion that Israel will abandon God and forfeit the land, Israel has only two solutions for being kept from despair. Either God must relax the terms of the covenant, making it possible for them to keep it, or should he choose to maintain his high and holy standards, he must then find some way to endow his people with the capacity for meeting them. To do the first, he will have to accommodate himself to a version of humanity that he never intended, a humanity that does not bear his own image of goodness and truth, justice and love. To do the latter—and this we'll only come to fully understand in our readings in the Gospel of John—he'll have to make great sacrifice.

Return is a drumbeat of this chapter. Return to God, and he will return to you! *Return* was the drumbeat of the prophets after Israel was cast into exile. It's a word that signals repentance, the leaving off of sin and coming back to God. In fact, *return* was at the center of a story that Jesus himself told of an aging father and a prodigal son.[3] Everything in that story changed when the wayward son, having squandered his inheritance, made a tentative return, if only as a desperate and hungry measure.

When he returned, he found his father—and a party—waiting for him.

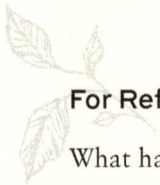

For Reflection/Discussion

What have been the results of trying to change on the basis of your own strength and willpower? What's so hopeful about the idea that God intends to "circumcise" our hearts?

DAY 18

Read Deuteronomy 31:1–30 (Focus: vv. 16–20)

Key Verse: "It is the Lord *your God who goes with you. . . . He will not leave you or forsake you."* (*v.* 6)

The With-God Life

In our recent move, I misplaced my journal. I don't write in it every day, so it took me about a week to miss it. And because the entries are hardly scandalous, I'm not worried about the hands those pages have fallen into. The entries usually begin with some mundane detail about how I slept, how cold the winter mornings have grown, how busy I'm feeling with work and family, how quietly the house purrs in the hours before dawn.

I thought of this lost journal when I heard an interview with Charles Moore, author of the three-volume authorized biography of Margaret Thatcher. Before her decline and death, Thatcher gave Moore access to all her papers and relinquished the right to review his work. I wondered about the revelations in all those pages and the gargantuan task of trying to make sense of a human life.

On the one hand, the words of Moses, recorded in the Pentateuch, take up more space in our Bibles than the words of anyone else, even Jesus. Yet for all these words, there is no authorized biography of his life. The papers he leaves behind, bound together in a scroll, aren't memoir. As we see in our reading today, Moses has copied the commandments that he received from God and passed on to the people, then given strict instruction about this book to the Levites and priests. They must place it beside the ark of the covenant and read it aloud every seventh year on the occasion of the national holiday called the Feast of Booths. This book will serve to teach future generations "to fear the LORD [their] God."

As we prepare to finish Deuteronomy, we're left with important questions having to do with Moses and his legacy. Was he an effective leader? Was he a failure? As we consider his story, we might also ask, What does it tell us about the bigger story God is writing—namely, the story of himself?

At the end of his life, Moses has nearly completed the task God gave him more than forty years earlier when he first appeared to him at the burning bush. At God's command, Moses bravely confronted Pharaoh; he led the nation out of Egypt and through the Red Sea. And though he hadn't signed up for forty years of wilderness wandering, levied because of the nation's faithlessness, Moses stuck with God's stubborn and sinful people. Even in Deuteronomy, as Israel stands poised on the border of the promised land, Moses continues to model pastoral diligence. He himself isn't getting into the land, but he's still preaching, still imploring the people to be faithful to God. If we were grading on the basis of effort alone, Moses as leader seems to deserve an A.

On the other hand, if Moses were called up for a performance review, there would be the question of measurable outcomes. However brilliantly his sermons have been delivered, God assures Moses that they will be blatantly ignored. Moses has shepherded God's people through the great and terrifying wilderness, but he hasn't been able to secure their spiritual safety. He can't guarantee their faithfulness to God. He has even fallen prey to his own mistrust and anger, and this is why he'll remain east of the Jordan, barred entry to the promised land.

I wonder what sense Moses tried making of his 120 years, 80 of them shaped by the wilderness.[1] I wonder whether there's resignation or peace to be found on his face as he nears the end of his life.

But maybe our takeaway is to think not of the relative failure or success of Moses's leadership with regard to Israel's fate. Perhaps we're meant to consider the example of faith he left. Before Moses was a leader and statesman, he was a friend of God.

In Exodus 33, we learn a little bit about the physical arrangement of the Israelite camp throughout their years of wandering. On the outskirts of the camp, Moses pitched a temporary structure he called the "Tent of Meeting." It's here that he and Joshua, Moses's successor, met regularly with God. Although it may have been a familiar sight for the people of Israel—these two men disappearing behind the curtain of the tent's entrance, the cloud descending to rest on its threshold—there was also something extraordinary about these conversations. It caused everyone in the camp to stand at the thresholds of their own tents in order to watch and worship.[2] We learn elsewhere that after each of these meetings, Moses retained a kind of afterglow, his face ablaze with the presence of God.[3]

Moses was a man who demonstrated that a life of faith is not something we do *for* God but a life we live *with* God. In fact, when God had threatened to abandon his people after the incident of the golden calf, allowing them to inherit the land but to lose his company, Moses knew that was no bargain to strike. If God did not go with them, the land would be a worthless gift.

Moses knew that at its very essence, faith means believing that God goes with his people, that he is a friend who will never leave or forsake. I imagine that part of what sustained Moses in the wilderness, as the people badgered him over lack of food and threatened to stone him when the water ran dry, was the comfort of knowing he wasn't alone. I think of him returning to that tent on the outskirts of camp, pouring out his trouble to the God who hears. Surely these experiences inform his commissioning speech for Joshua, when he tells him to be strong and courageous, not to fear or be in dread. I don't think Moses meant to diminish the threats that lay ahead of Joshua and the people so much as to reassure them that God's going with them would make all the difference.

I don't want to give the impression that the life of faith is easier than a life without faith. No, there are still haunting worries that rouse believers from sleep, still regrets we nurse from the past, still the ever-present harrow of death. We can feel small in this world and frightened by our smallness. The invitation of faith isn't to pretend that there aren't big, bad scary wolves; that life can't wreck with a sudden change of weather; that we don't feel angry or sad or disappointed—even occasionally abandoned. But it is to say that we keep at the habit of believing the improbable: we're not left or forsaken; God is *with* us.

By faith we keep believing that we're befriended.

For Reflection/Discussion

What do you take away from Moses's legacy in the book of Deuteronomy? What would change about your habits of faith if you thought of faith less as intellectual knowledge and more as friendship with God?

DAY 19

Read Deuteronomy 32:1–52 (Focus: vv. 1–6)

Key Verse: "You were unmindful of the Rock that bore you, and you forgot the God who gave you birth." (v. 18)

The Laboring God

It has been a bumpy year of parenting. We launched our first child into the overtures of adulthood, and though she has confidently landed on her feet, the severing has been harder than forecasted. I have felt as tentative in this season as in the earliest days of motherhood. I don't know how to parent someone who is clearly fine, on most days, doing without me. I don't like admitting my grief at the extended periods of silence between us. I want to refuse the role of nagging mother, but her clamorous voice is hard to silence.

I confessed this to a friend who is launching her own adult children into the world. "They won't learn to appreciate us without us teaching them," my friend said emphatically. We both shared the feeling, right or wrong, that a debt was owed to us by our children. We both admitted how we hated begging for gratitude.

These are the thoughts I bring with me into Deuteronomy 32—where God likens himself to a laboring mother. Of course, there are other images of God in this chapter: God as rock, the safe, unyielding, fixed point of protection; God as father, the creator and sustainer; God as eagle mother, hovering over her young and sheltering them under her pinions. But as a mother who has given birth five times, I'm arrested by the image of God as a pregnant mother in the middle of delivering her baby. This is, in fact, the vivid language of verse 18 in the Hebrew: "The Rock who gave birth to you, who writhed in labor to bear you." Moses's words call to mind the words of another prophet and his use of the image of God as laboring woman: "Now I will cry out like a woman in labor; I will gasp and pant."[1] To think of God as a laboring woman is to think of the cord by which humanity was once joined to God, to remember how we had suckled our very life from God. It is also to imagine God's pain at the severing of that belonging, to think of the grief God suffers when God's children remain estranged, calling only when they need money.

As we near the end of Deuteronomy, we see in bold relief what beats at the heart of this book, indeed what beats at the heart of the Bible. It's the unrequited love of God and the debt of gratitude owed to him by humanity. As Moses puts it in the words of this song meant for memorializing the people's unfaithfulness: "Do you thus repay the LORD, you foolish and senseless people?" The people of God stand on the precipice of inheriting the good land promised to Abraham many generations earlier. They stand to inherit benefits for which they've borne no burdens: houses and fields, olive groves and vineyards. Their history tells the story of God's constant favor, how despite their chronic failure, he delivered them from Egypt and provided for them in the wilderness.

Indeed, to go back even further, their history begs them to remember the very beginning of time itself as recorded in the first book of the Pentateuch, the book of Genesis. When the world was yet a wilderness, God spoke light into darkness. Out of the formless void, he made a habitable world and spread a feast before his children, begging them to eat. To read the Bible, there can be no doubting God's generosity—and no doubting that we have spurned it. As Hebrew scholar Robert Alter poetically translates verse 5: "Did [God] act ruinously? No, his sons' the fault—A perverse and twisted brood."[2]

In his classic work *Mere Christianity*, C. S. Lewis writes that it's important to understand the questions that Christianity looks to answer rather than insist it always answer our own particular curiosities. His advice proves a helpful way of transitioning from our reading of the book of Deuteronomy to our reading of the Gospel of John. As readers, we might puzzle over the questions Deuteronomy leaves us with—and that John may look to answer.

Here are a couple of questions I could suggest. First, noting the contrast highlighted in this song taught to the people—that God is perfect, just, and upright, lacking no moral fault; that his people are blemished and twisted, lacking understanding—maybe the question is, What's to be done about humanity's moral crookedness in light of God's straight line? Second, noting the apparent gap as the song concludes—between God giving his people up and surrendering them to the disasters of their own making, and then vindicating them and rousing himself to compassion and vengeance on their behalf—maybe the question is, What changes God's mind?[3]

The book of Deuteronomy has clearly put the habit of obedience at the very center of our love for God. God's people are called, time and again, to moral "carefulness," to an exacting diligence about their spiritual lives. However, for all the strictness of God's commands, Deuteronomy emphasizes that God's people are not capable of meeting God's standards. They are crooked arrows shot from bent bows. The problem, as far as we see it in Deuteronomy, is not one of genetics, not one of environment, not one of education, not one of economics. It is not an external problem at all, but a corruption of the heart—a problem requiring outside intervention.

This pronouncement of spiritual sickness could seem harsh and unwelcome. But at the beginning of his song, Moses employs images that reveal the true life-giving nature of his words. They are dew and rain, showers and cloudbursts. They fall on the hard-baked clay of the human heart, bearing with them all the possibility of life. They don't kill but resuscitate. Moses's words are the very wounds of a friend mentioned in the wisdom literature of the Bible.[4] Love can sometimes feel severe.

Perhaps we could see our own hearts as this hard-baked clay. Perhaps we could begin accepting responsibility for our moral crookedness. Perhaps we could tell God that we are a twisted people, bent and crooked and in need of a miracle.

Perhaps this is the first step required for those who want to *live*.

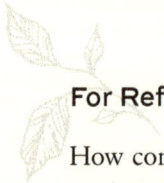

For Reflection/Discussion

How convinced are you that your moral and spiritual problems are internal, not external? Practically, how could you take up the habit of confessing your moral crookedness to God and asking for his grace?

DAY 20

Read Deuteronomy 33:1–34:12 (Focus: 34:1–12)

Key Verse: "This is the blessing with which Moses the man of God blessed the people of Israel before his death." (33:1)

The Bookends of Blessing

I was reading cancer memoirs this spring for a book review assignment. It was hardly the depressing task it might seem. I read Paul Kalanithi's *When Breath Becomes Air*, marveling that he and his wife chose to have a child despite knowing he would not live to see her grow up. I read Nina Rigg's *The Bright Hour*, my eyes blurring when she anticipated the grief of leaving ordinary things undone: "the unplayed voicemails, the unwalked dogs; uncollapsed recycling . . . universe coming undone at the seams."[1] I read Julie Yip-Williams's *The Unwinding of the Miracle*, hearing her frank anger at her full cup of suffering. "Life is not fair," she wrote in the letter for her young daughters. "You would be foolish to expect fairness."[2]

Each of the stories is finished in an epilogue by their partners, and each is a poignant reminder of the truth of Psalm 90, which is attributed to Moses and reminds us of the brevity of our lives. We are grass that flourishes in the morning and fades in the evening. We are made of dust, and to dust we shall return. Mortality is the human sentence. But there is more to this ancient prayer song than resignation or anger. Instead, Moses seeks to live well in life's fading light. "Teach us to number our days that we may get a heart of wisdom."[3] In prayer, he looks to the only one capable of endowing such a gift. The confidence of Psalm 90 is in the eternal God.

As we finish the book of Deuteronomy today, we find Moses at the end of his 120 years of "toil and trouble."[4] This final scene, where Moses surveys the breadth of the promised land, calls to mind an earlier scene in Genesis 13. Abraham had just arrived in Canaan, only to realize that the land of promise would not support his household and that of his nephew. Forced to part ways, Abraham gives the first pick of the land to Lot. Lot travels east, toward the lush Jordan Valley. Abraham remains in Canaan, and God invites Abraham to lift up his eyes and survey the land, northward and southward and eastward and westward. "All the land that you see I will give to you and to your offspring forever."[5] God invited Abraham, like Moses, to survey the proportions of his promise.

These two scenes form what scholars call an *inclusio*. Acting like a pair of literary bookends, an inclusio hems in the narrative. Here, this particular inclusio hems in the entire Pentateuch and functions to draw our attention to the promise of the land. At the end of his life, Abraham did not see God's promise fulfilled in its entirety. Rather, he owned just a small burial plot at the time of his death. Similarly, as the curtains of his life draw to a close, Moses is also invited to see the land but not to possess it.

Some would say that this literary inclusio highlights the nature of faith, how it's forged in liminal places, when God's promises act like promissory notes. Faith requires us to take God at his word, even when the reality of our lives seems to suggest that such trust is misplaced. Faith is about hoping in the unseen, about remaining confident in what's yet to come.[6]

Another scene may yet be in mind here for the author/editors of Deuteronomy. At the end of the book of Genesis, after Jacob's family has been resettled in the land of Egypt because of famine and before Jacob's death, the patriarch gathers his sons (and two of his grandsons) around his deathbed. Naming each tribe, he confers on them his blessing. To Joseph, he speaks the bounties of the everlasting hills: "May they be on the head of Joseph, and on the brow of him who was set apart from his brothers."[7] Many hundreds of years later, Moses speaks strikingly familiar words when he names the favored son of Joseph: may "the best gifts of the earth and its fullness . . . rest on the head of Joseph, on the pate of him who is prince among his brothers." Blessing is the rich inheritance of God's people, passed from father to son, from leader to people.

The final words of Moses to Israel are blessing, not curse.

This should surprise us, given how much weight of the book has been devoted to the curses, given how resigned the book is to the moral unreliability of God's people. Deuteronomy doesn't leave us to wonder about the future for Israel. What's clear is that Israel will betray the covenant and forfeit the land. But in spite of this prediction, Moses proves strangely hopeful about their future. "Happy are you, O Israel!" What accounts for his optimism?

Perhaps there is one more inclusio to consider that will help us to answer that question. It's the blessing with which the Pentateuch opens, in the very first chapter of Genesis. When God made the world and welcomed humanity into it, his very first words were a pronouncement of blessing. "And God blessed them. And God said to them, 'Be fruitful and multiply and fill the earth and subdue it.'"[8] The Pentateuch opens with blessing in Genesis and closes with blessing in Deuteronomy, perhaps as if to demonstrate how irrepressible God's generosity really is. His love might be spurned by his children, but he will bless them still—because it's part of his character to shower favor. The blessing of God has nothing to do with the worthiness of those who are blessed. It has everything to do with his own bigheartedness.

This, I think, is what underlies the "happiness" of faith, as Moses calls it. If we had to earn God's love by flawless moral performance and spiritual steadfastness, we would be fated to be a deeply unhappy people. As the apostle Paul writes in his letter to the Romans, we suffer from inner contradiction and do not do as we intend. "For I do not understand my own actions. For I do not do what I want, but I do the very thing I hate. . . . Who will deliver me from this body of death?"[9] But if, on the other hand, we are mercifully received by God in spite of our moral contradictions, we are rescued from guilt and shame. There is no longer condemnation but freedom. This isn't, of course, the freedom to abuse his kindness. Faith is the freedom to respond wholeheartedly to it. It's the freedom to seize the blessings.

It's the freedom to *live*.

For Reflection/Discussion

As we end our reading of Deuteronomy, what's one insight about the habits of faith that you'll take with you into our reading of John? What's one question?

MIKA EDMONDSON

"If you will save me, then I will live for you."

Mika Edmondson grew up in the housing projects of East Nashville. His maternal grandparents, formerly sharecroppers in Alabama, had moved to Nashville to escape the violence of racism in the Deep South. His father, a factory worker, and his mother, a nurse, occasionally took Mika and his brother to Mount Gilead Missionary Baptist Church, where his grandmother—"the matriarch of the family and a real prayer warrior"—was a prominent member of the congregation.

"Back then, I would have said that I was a Christian because I had an affiliation with the church and because I knew some Sunday school stories. But I didn't have a vital relationship with Jesus, even though I prayed every night and had an awareness of the reality that God exists, that God is big." Mika recounted the fear struck in his heart after watching a movie depicting the rapture—when Christians suddenly disappear from the earth and unbelievers are subject to intense suffering. "It was meant to invoke fear, and it did its job. That seeded in my mind [ideas about] God's greatness and the fierceness of God's wrath. I knew that there was a judgment coming on this world because of sin."

At a young age, Mika had the chance to leave his failing elementary school and attend a magnet school. As a result, his academic trajectory changed dramatically, and he eventually earned a presidential scholarship to college where he chose to study physics. His first years of college were, as he described them, a period of "social respectability." Earning good grades, he was a paragon of achievement in his family. "Again, if you'd asked me, I would have said I believed in Jesus. But I was thinking about how I could further my own aims, my own ambitions in life."

Externally, Mika had a life to be envied. Internally, however, he knew that things were amiss. "I struggled with insecurity, with impatience, with anger. The Lord let me start to see my own internal brokenness." On one particular visit home from college during his sophomore year, Mika recalled how he'd become agitated with his mother and raised his voice at her. "That was a big no-no in our family structure, and it was a low for me. I realized that I didn't have the self-restraint not to [act on my anger]." He began to admit to himself, *Something's really wrong, and I'm powerless to change*. Mika knew that anger had become a deep-seated pattern in his life and that he couldn't simply will it away.

In this season of personal reckoning, a friend in Mika's physics cohort, who was also a pastor at a local Pentecostal church, invited him to a revival meeting. *Why not?* Mika thought. *It's the respectable thing to do*. When he arrived, fewer than twenty people were gathered. The church building was small, composed of only two rooms. The meeting started with a lot of fervent prayer and Scripture reading. Forty-five minutes later, a man wearing a long trench coat strode through the door and up to the front where he kicked off his shoes and started to sing. Eventually, the song became a sermon, whose title Mika remembered as "Spiritual Organized Crime."

Prophet Morris, as the man was called, preached on the text of 2 Samuel 11, where King David takes Bathsheba to sleep with him though she is married to another man. When she becomes pregnant and David cannot coax Bathsheba's husband, Uriah, from the battlefield to enjoy his conjugal privileges, David has Uriah killed. Prophet Morris explained that in this familiar story, Satan had set up David to take the fall—but that God's grace was greater than anything the devil had planned. "In the midst of [Prophet Morris speaking], I got a sense of the Lord's persistent grace," Mika said. "He can save the worst of sinners, I realized. I got an awareness that despite all my social respectability, I was broken and in need of God's salvation." At that moment, Mika called out to the Lord: "If you will save me, then I will live for you."

"I was confronted with grace that claimed me. In that moment, I knew that Jesus had always been for me, that he had been at work in my life even when I was rebelling against him and rejecting him. All the gospel that I had neglected or ignored as a child came flooding back in my mind. Jesus had been the one pursuing me the entire time. He had apprehended me, and I surrendered out of gratitude. His grace appeared to me to be a solid certainty in the midst of a lot of uncertainty. It appeared to be the thing that gave me security in the midst of the fear of my brokenness."

At that same revival meeting, Prophet Morris spoke predictions about Mika's future: he would marry the young girl he'd attended the meeting with; he'd enter vocational ministry. Christina did in fact become his wife one week after their college graduation, and a year and a half into a PhD in astronomy at the University of Rochester, Mika abandoned science for theology. One of his advisors at the time warned that his decision was ill-advised: "You can probably be more faithful to your community as an African American if you're an astronomer," he tried persuading. "There are black preachers everywhere." But Mika felt certain of his call. "Whatever intellect I had, I wanted to use it for the kingdom in the way of formal ministry."

Mika Edmondson is a Presbyterian pastor and church planter. He earned a doctorate in systematic theology from Calvin Seminary and is the author of The Power of Unearned Suffering, *a book about Martin Luther King's theology of suffering.*

DAY 21

Read John 1:1–51 (Focus: vv. 14–18)

Key Verse: "For the law was given through Moses; grace and truth came through Jesus Christ." (v. 17)

Where We Left Off

As the mother of twins, I'm constantly amazed that two human beings, sharing such proximity from conception, can be so vastly different. This past Christmas, one of the twins asked for a smartwatch for Christmas. "I'll run every day," he insisted, enticing me to consider the energy he would burn in timed loops around our block. The other twin asked for books.

Our bibliophile burns through books like his brother burns calories. At breakfast one morning, another novel in hand, this twin asked me: "Do you think the title of the book should be bigger, or the title of the series?" He preferred the latter. Diplomatically, I confessed that I couldn't decide.

There's something rewarding about discovering connections across titles in a book series. In one way, this is part of the thrill of reading the Gospel of John. Although a new story is beginning in Jesus, a much older one is also continuing. As we discover in our first reading from this Gospel, John intentionally borrows from Old Testament melodic lines.

As one obvious connection, the Gospel of John opens with a recognizable motif from the book of Genesis: "In the beginning." Before God spoke the world into being and called light from darkness, Jesus, the eternal Word, existed. He was speaking. In fact, the universe has never been silent—because the Word of God has always been. Because Jesus is God, he is without beginning and end.

This reference to Jesus as the "Word" of God hearkens back to Deuteronomy, whose Hebrew title means, "These are the words." We learned that the God who *is* is the God who *speaks*, that the God who *speaks* is the God who *loves*. When Moses climbed Mount Sinai, disappearing into the thick cloud of God's transcendence, and God spoke his law to his people, it was a merciful expression of his willingness to be known. Even after Israel plugged their ears and committed the treachery forecast in Deuteronomy, God continued speaking. John the Evangelist now bears witness to this "grace upon grace"—that despite his people's deafness, God hasn't been easily dissuaded from his speaking.

According to verse 18, Jesus is God's enfleshed sermon. All that God is, all that God wills, all that God hates, all that God longs to accomplish—these can be understood in the person of Jesus Christ. Where a book like Deuteronomy leaves us suspended, fumbling in the fog of our own dim understanding, wondering how God will bless his accursed people, John's proclamation of Jesus Christ arrives like a radiant dawn. All that came before "in the Law and also the prophets" laid down clues for puzzling out the climactic event of God moving into the neighborhood—but it did not fully detail how the story would unfold. The Hebrew Bible was a foreshadowing, its meaning only fully illuminated by the events of Jesus's life, death, and resurrection.

In theological terms, Christians refer to this coming of God in the flesh as the incarnation. It proves God's preference not for the abstract but the concrete, not for the conceptual but the corporeal. Christian faith, in other words, is not a grappling with ideas about God. Instead, it's an encounter with—and surrender to—the living, speaking God of Jesus Christ: the God to be seen and touched and heard. As the Evangelist tells us at the end of his Gospel, John hasn't written simply to convey information about this Jesus. Rather, he wants us to believe in Jesus as the Christ, the Sent One, the Son of God—and to have *life* in his name.[1] *Welcome* might be the best word (even better than *believe*) for conveying the activity of faith.[2]

It's a mystery how the eternal, timeless, infinite God squeezed himself into a mortal human body. Other religions, such as Islam, see the incarnation as a great affront to God's majesty. Even early Christians struggled to articulate the mechanics of God made flesh and debated the details over several centuries in the councils of Nicaea, Constantinople, and Chalcedon. Eventually, it was agreed that this truth—Jesus, fully God, fully man—must be resolutely affirmed as a paradox: a mind-bending both/and.

As we begin our reading of this Gospel, we can affirm the historical reliability of the text that we have before us. It's been popular, of course, to convey the four canonical Gospels—Matthew, Mark, Luke, and John—as biased, unreliable accounts of Jesus's life, written generations after his death from the fallible memory of his disciples.[3] Infamously, the Jesus Seminar, founded by Richard W. Funk in 1985, assembled a group of scholars in order to find the "truth" of the historical Jesus. Funk memorably opened the group's first meeting with the fiery pronouncement that "a rude and rancorous awakening" lay ahead.[4] He was sure their scholarship would rend historic Christian faith and leave it in tatters. But despite his predictions, many scholars continue to find defensible reasons for affirming the historicity of the four Gospels: their fundamental assertions about Jesus, the early dating of existing fragments, the multiplicity of manuscripts.

As historians, the Gospel writers had a vested interest in getting their stories right. Of course they had interpretative decisions to make about what to omit, what to include, what to emphasize, and what to footnote, and theirs was a task of selectivity. As they sifted through reliable source material—including eyewitness testimony—they crafted a narrative that made sense of the facts they gathered. And because each of the Gospel writers had different literary purposes, different theological aims, none of the Gospels reads as a facsimile of another. In fact, of the four, John's Gospel is the most different. John leaves out important episodes, such as the baptism of Jesus, the temptation of Jesus, the exorcisms that Jesus performed, and the parables that Jesus taught. He also uniquely includes other events: Jesus's first miracle at the wedding at Cana, his late-night meeting with the Pharisee Nicodemus, and his noonday conversation with a Samaritan woman.

Still, like the other three Gospel writers, John wants to call his readers to a personal encounter with the Word—Jesus Christ of Nazareth. He invites them, as Jesus himself did, to "come and see." There's no propaganda in his account—and no hint of coercion. There's simply this: the invitation to dip our toes into the water of faith and reckon with the evidence of God made flesh.

Faith can begin with as simple a habit as curiosity.

For Reflection/Discussion

What's most intriguing to you about the identity of Jesus as illuminated in this chapter: that he is the Word, the Creator, the eternal God, the Life, the Light—or simply a human being? What will it mean for you to respond in the days to come to Jesus's invitation to "come and see"?

DAY 22

Read John 2:1–25 (Focus: vv. 23–25)

Key Verse: "Many believed in his name when they saw the signs that he was doing." (v. 23)

That Wine Will Preach

"That's the most fun I've ever had without alcohol." My husband's grandfather, hardly a teetotaler, was impressed that our wedding reception had been as lively as it was dry. (In 1996, we might have credited some of that good, sober humor to the Macarena.)

Both my husband and I were raised in dry households. There wasn't wine in the fridge or booze in the kitchen cabinet—not even for the innocuous purpose of making pie crust or pasta sauce. It took years (and multiple children) before we ever dared serve wine at a holiday dinner with extended family. Both of us attended a conservative Christian college where we pledged, as many generations did before us, to abstain from alcohol during school terms.

In certain religious communities, the tradition of temperance has been long. That can make it difficult, for some, to understand the nature of Jesus's first miracle. Wine for wedding guests already on their way to getting drunk? Surely there would have been better miracles for launching Jesus into public ministry, miracles that would have satisfied real needs and promoted him as a proper religious figure. Surely there was a famine to end somewhere in the world.

But as we reflected yesterday, everything is purposeful in John's account. There's nothing accidental about this party appearing at the very beginning of his account of Jesus's public ministry. For a Gospel that began with the cosmic, esoteric declaration "In the beginning was the Word," John 2 is a quick and jerky descent. Here we have a Jesus who is as earthy as he is eternal. He's not a ghostly, gauzy figure from another planet. He attends weddings. His mother expects regular phone calls.

John's account of the wedding at Cana takes a sledgehammer to the divide that we've often erected between the sacred and the secular, the spiritual and the ordinary. Although Christians have a long and unfortunate history of making every pleasure a guilty one, this narrative doesn't tolerate asceticism for its own sake. No, it tells us that God can be as comfortable at a party as he is in the church pew—that our habits of faith can be as celebratory as they are contemplative.

Of course, the wedding of Cana is no admonition to "eat and drink, for tomorrow we die,"[1] and the Bible doesn't condone drunkenness. Still, wine belonged to a trinity of promises that God had made to Israel. When Israel was exiled from the good land it had inherited by faith, the prophets spoke hopefully of the "grain" and "wine" and "oil" that God would restore to his people when they returned home.[2] Even earlier still, when the patriarch Jacob laid hands of blessing on each of his sons before his death, he pronounced that the clothes of Judah (the tribe from which Jesus would descend) would be soaked in wine.[3] The fulfillment of these Torah promises—of God's return to his people, of his people returning home—was signaled at the wedding at Cana. This wasn't just another boozy party. It was a wine-soaked proclamation of God's faithfulness.

Unlike other Gospel writers who prefer the language of "miracle" for the spectacular events in Jesus's ministry, John calls this water-turned-wine the first of many "signs" by which God's luminous glory would shine through Jesus and cause people to believe.[4] In fact, there were other signs that Jesus was performing in Jerusalem, and as John records, people did see and believe. However, there's something about this "faith" of the crowds that Jesus found tenuous, reminding us of previous lessons in Deuteronomy.

As you'll remember, Moses reminded the nation of Israel again and again of God's great "power and outstretched arm." He constantly recounted the "signs and wonders" that God performed on their behalf: the ten plagues of disaster on Egypt, the parting of the Red Sea, water from a rock, manna from heaven. Israel had ample evidence for God's reality as well as God's goodness. But these "signs" were never entirely sufficient for faith, at least not for the kind of faith that persevered through difficulty. In fact, Israel's craving for the material and the visible proved to be a way of skirting faith rather than supporting it. (If we're honest, we all beg for proof.)

The apostle Paul addressed human incredulity in one of his letters to the church in Corinth:[5] "For Jews demand signs and Greeks seek wisdom, but we preach Christ crucified, a stumbling block to Jews and folly to Gentiles, but to those who are called, both Jews and Greeks, Christ the power of God and the wisdom of God."[6] The only subversive proof Paul was willing to offer on behalf of Jesus was his gruesome death on a cross.

From these earliest chapters, John is shaping his biography of Jesus in light of the final events of Jesus's life: his death and resurrection. For one, the wedding at Cana is purported to have taken place "on the third day." Having no indication about this day's relationship within a larger context of time (the week? the month?), we can credibly assume that John is thinking about the final *third day*: the Easter Sunday following the first Good Friday. This wedding party is a foreshadowing of a greater cosmic celebration: when God abandoned his graveclothes and strode out of his tomb, dealing a death blow to death itself.

Signs and wonders were given to Israel as well as to those in Jesus's generation—but they did not ensure lasting faith. It didn't matter how many times God dazzled them with fantastic displays of power. Every new crisis was a new reason to disbelieve. This puts a squirmy question to all of us when we think of our own hesitant spiritual journeys. Is it evidence we lack—or faith? In other words, are we wrongly expecting to turn some future corner when, all our questions having been answered, faith will no longer be required? Given the choice, would we demand certainty over trust?

There is no day, for the Christian, that doesn't oblige us to faith. It takes faith to believe that God has come in Jesus, faith to believe that all the Jewish Scriptures written before Jesus point to him, faith to believe that all the Gospels written about Jesus provide reliable accounts of his life, especially his death and resurrection.

It takes faith to keep following Jesus—even when the lights go dark.

For Reflection/Discussion

What drives your quest for certainty in matters of faith? When have you had to exercise faith apart from any visible signs of God's reality?

DAY 23

Read John 3:1–36 (Focus: vv. 13–17)

Key Verse: "For God so loved the world, that he gave his only Son, that whoever believes in him should not perish but have eternal life." (v. 16)

On Getting Fidgety

When we moved to Toronto in 2011, we quickly realized how "fundamentalist" we seemed to our neighbors. (This wasn't helped by the fact that we had five children.) I remember catching up with a neighbor one morning as we walked our kids to school. After the conversation turned to faith and he glimpsed how central Jesus was to our lives, he said to me, half-bemused, "I've known a couple of born-agains like you."

I don't usually call myself a born-again Christian. Even though it's a phrase Jesus himself used, I've feared that at its worst *born again* conjures images of snake handlers and street preachers with bullhorns, and that at its best *born again* suggests an obliviousness to Seinfeld references.

In our passage today, Jesus tells Nicodemus that he must be "born again." This must have caught this Pharisee by surprise. If anyone was religiously serious, it was Nicodemus.[1] He was a fundamentalist of his day—fastidious in his handwashing, in his handling of food, in his sacrificial offerings at the temple. No doubt he wore the Jewish Scriptures on his body and recited Jewish prayers at prescribed times throughout the day. Likely he had long-winded sections of Deuteronomy committed to heart.

In his conversation with Nicodemus, Jesus wastes no time in correcting one of the most insidious misconceptions about faith. He insists that it's not religious résumés that impress God. No, God isn't recruiting straight-A religious types who spit-polish their shoes. As we saw in Deuteronomy, the only thing that's reliably true about human beings is their inability to be faithful to God. To be born again is to admit that the first step toward grace is an empty-handed one. It's to understand that God isn't simply looking to improve his people—but to re-create them, in the language of the apostle Paul.[2]

To be born again is to know this: the only thing we need in a life with God is neediness.

Spiritual rebirth, as Jesus explains, happens by virtue of a baptism of "water" and the "Spirit." These might seem like cryptic ideas, but this language returns us to a very familiar promise in the writings of the prophets.[3] After Israel had rebelled against God and been exiled from the promised land, the prophet Ezekiel wrote of God's willingness to restore his wayward children: "I will sprinkle clean water on you, and you shall be clean from all your uncleannesses, and from all your idols I will cleanse you. And I will give you a new heart, and a new spirit I will put within you. And I will remove the heart of stone from your flesh and give you a heart of flesh. And I will put my Spirit within you and cause you to walk in my statutes and be careful to obey my rules."[4] Speaking both of cleansing water and the gift of a new spirit, Ezekiel's prophecy suggested the solution to the problem posed in Deuteronomy—this problem of the straight line of God's law and the moral crookedness of the human heart. Ezekiel has anticipated that the law wouldn't be relaxed. Rather, the human heart would be straightened, reformed, made new.

The Gospel writer John sees this solution as tied inextricably—and exclusively—to the person and work of Jesus Christ, in whom we can be "born of water and the Spirit." It's here, of course, that we can find ourselves getting fidgety. Can't we just agree that there are many paths to God—and that Jesus represents one such way? As one parable from an ancient Hindu text teaches, perhaps all world religions are really just our fumbling attempts in the dark to understand the nature of God. In our human blindness, maybe we can only draw partial conclusions about divine reality. Maybe God is like an elephant: I grab his trunk and take him for a snake; you grab his ear and take him for a fan; another grabs his tusk and takes him for a spear. But as Rebecca McLaughlin writes in *Confronting Christianity*, this analogy doesn't grapple with the consequential differences between Hinduism and Christianity, between Islam and Judaism, between New Age spirituality and Buddhism.[5] Further, it makes faith a blind sport of best guess. It relativizes all human knowledge of God.

This is emphatically *not* the message of John. John says that God sent a Word, an enfleshed sermon, to teach us what God is like. We are not blindly fumbling in the dark. Rather, we've been given *Light*! And while Christianity makes a claim about the *uniqueness* of Jesus Christ, it also makes a claim about the *universality* of God's love.[6] According to verse 16 (surely the most televised verse in the Bible), God loved the entire world so much that he *gave* Jesus. "*Whoever* believes in him"—the lecher, the pill-popper, the prostitute, the liar, the smug, the self-righteous, the hypocrite—"should not perish but have eternal life" (emphasis added). God has already persevered long in his generosity toward ungrateful Israel, and now he has given one final, lavish, liberal, free gift. He has given himself.

It's not hard to measure what this giving cost God. As we'll see at the end of John's Gospel, it cost him betrayal by one of his disciples. It cost him abandonment by his closest friends. It cost him rejection by his family. It cost him excruciating torture and public humiliation before it ultimately cost him his very life. It begs us to ask, What did God spare in his love for this world? For you? For me?

This is the heart of the Christian gospel: God is the giver of every good gift, and his best gift is Jesus. The most important habit of faith is to stretch out our hands and to believe this gift is for us—apart from anything we'd ever do to deserve it. Because gratefully, in the Gospel of John, "believe" is a verb that's never modified by *truly* or *deeply* or *faithfully*. It's not a work we perform but a promise we trust.

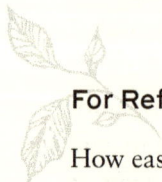

For Reflection/Discussion

How easy is it for you to believe in God's generous love for you? How readily do you see your own need for the heart transplant that Ezekiel wrote about—and the rebirth that Jesus spoke of?

DAY 24

Read John 4:1–54 (Focus: vv. 23–26)

Key Verses: "The Father is seeking such people to worship him . . . in spirit and truth." (vv. 23–24)

A Ringing World of Praise

I've previously mentioned Macina, the small, arid town on the northern banks of the Niger River where we five college students and a Ghanaian couple spent the summer. Because the rains were late in coming, it was all the more obvious how precious water was to the people of Macina. Central to every day's activities were our frequent trips to the well near our compound. We went two by two, needing four hands to carry back the large basins of water used for cooking, "flushing" the toilets, and keeping ourselves as clean as the sweltering heat would allow. When it was laundry day, the young woman we had hired to scrub our clothes worked beside the well, drying our American T-shirts (and underwear) in the blinding sun.

In the Pentateuch, wells are a frequent setting for much of the dramatic action. To own access to water was to ensure survival. As Hebrew scholar Robert Alter points out, the Hebrew Bible makes frequent use of a particular literary type-scene, which he calls "the encounter with the future betrothed at the well."[1] In this scene, a future bridegroom travels to a foreign land and encounters a girl (or group of girls) beside a well. Someone draws water from the well, the girls rush home to bring news of the stranger's arrival, and the betrothal of the stranger and one of the girls is concluded with an invitation to a meal.[2]

John's account of Jesus's acquaintance with the Samaritan woman bears similarity to this Old Testament type-scene. John has already primed our imaginative pump by including a wedding story close to the beginning of his Gospel, and in Jesus's conversation with the Samaritan woman, the subject turns, rather abruptly, to her many husbands. Jesus, a Jew, has entered the foreign land of the Samaritans, which many Jews of his day took great travel pains to avoid.[3] Finally, at the end of the Samaritan woman's conversation with Jesus, she hastily forgets her water jar and hurries to tell everyone in town about the stranger's arrival. "Can this be the Christ?"

Importantly, we can't ignore that in this story, the "gift of God" is available to someone who is the cultural "other." People often assume that Christianity is "White" and "Western," but it has actually proven to be the most multicultural, multiracial, multiethnic movement in history. From its inception, Christianity has unified people from diverse socioeconomic strata, hostile political ideologies, and ethnic differences.

Christianity continues to be a globally diverse movement. In fact, Iran has the fastest-growing Christian movement in the world, and some predict that China will be a majority Christian country by 2050.[4] While it's true that "salvation is from the Jews" (because Jesus is a Jew), God is actively seeking worshipers from every nation, every tribe, and every tongue. He is not partial to the rich, to the educated, to the literate, to the politically progressive. Because Jesus stands in broad daylight, scandalously talking to a Samaritan woman, he proves how wide, how deep, how high God's love is for humanity.

If John really means to say that Jesus is the bridegroom—and this Samaritan woman, the bride—much of what we call the "gospel," or good news, comes into clearer focus. To see Jesus as the bridegroom is to learn about the nature of worship. It's not a perfunctory rite or ritual we perform on Sundays. It's a response of love, of ardent affection, of full-bodied appreciation and praise. Just as we learned from Deuteronomy that the greatest obligation we owe to God is to love him with all of our heart, all of our soul, all of our mind, all of our strength, John is thrusting Jesus forward as the one to whom all that love is owed. "I am he," Jesus tells the Samaritan woman: the one the prophets have foretold and the one your hearts have longed for. Look no further. I've come to satisfy the yearning of every human heart.

Perhaps we think it strange, as C. S. Lewis did upon becoming a Christian, that God would command this "perpetual eulogy." Why should God be so interested in making sure that humanity *worships* him? But Lewis soon realized how the world "rings with praise," how praise is the ordinary response we make to something inherently valuable. If God is the "supremely beautiful and all-satisfying Object," no other response but praise would make sense.[5] What's more, writes Lewis, praise completes our enjoyment of whatever we find praiseworthy. In other words, praise is for God—but it's also for us. When we worship God, instead of barren, fragile things that can never really satisfy, our hearts find their deepest rest and joy.

Jesus conveys these promises to the Samaritan woman in the language of water. We don't have to think hard about the great gift that water was to the Israelites in their forty years of wilderness wandering. In fact, Jewish legend may have taught that a real physical rock followed Israel in the wilderness, and that it was this rock that Moses struck twice that gushed forth water. (Other versions say that it wasn't a rock that followed Israel but an actual well.) The apostle Paul himself gives a name to the source of water from which Israel drank on their way to the promised land: "For [Israel] drank from the spiritual Rock that followed them, and the Rock was Christ."[6]

To be human is to be thirsty, and Jesus calls his followers to come and drink.

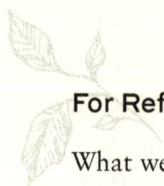

For Reflection/Discussion

What wells do you find yourself constantly drawing from without ever quenching your thirst? What difference would it make to believe not simply that Jesus is the Christ but also that Jesus is God's Living Water?

DAY 25

Read John 5:1–47 (Focus: vv. 39–47)

Key Verse: "For if you believed Moses, you would believe me; for he wrote of me." (v. 46)

The Great Mystery

It was a blustery January day, and I agreed to see *Knives Out* with my teenage daughter a second time. I rarely watch newly released movies, and even more rarely do I pay to see them twice in the theater. But this comedic murder mystery was memorable, and I looked forward to having the end in mind as I began again at the beginning.

Most of the time, I'm too impatient for the detective work that mystery requires. This past summer, after I'd borrowed Anthony Horowitz's *The Magpie Murders* from the library, I'd breathlessly finished it over a holiday weekend, turning pages at breakneck speed to solve the question of *whodunnit*.

Twentieth-century British writer G. K. Chesterton compared the gospel to a mystery story—and Jesus Christ to the intelligible moment when the mystery was finally solved. From Abraham to Moses to the prophets, God had provided clues that would finally puzzle together in the picture of Jesus. Abraham's faith had foreshadowed the believing in Jesus that John so insistently calls his readers to. Israel's failure had illuminated humanity's need for something more than the Mosaic law—and anticipated salvation through Jesus, who brought "grace upon grace." The prophets' unfailing hope—that God would dwell again with his people—was fully realized when God was made flesh and moved into the neighborhood. Everything written before Jesus in the law and the prophets was finally made clear in the events of his birth, life, death, and resurrection.

These connections between Jesus and the Old Testament stories and prophecies were hardly apparent to everyone living in John's day. The Jewish leaders rejected Jesus precisely because he did not conform to their expectations for the Messiah. For one, Jesus seemed to them an egregious Sabbath breaker, and keeping the Sabbath was one of the "big ten" in Mosaic law. It was a rule rooted in two of Israel's most important stories. Sabbath observance pointed back to creation, when God made the world in six days and rested on the seventh. Sabbath observance also pointed to the story of the exodus, when Israel was delivered out of Egyptian slavery. This weekly day of rest was one way in which the Jews practiced their distinctive identity as God's free people, made in his image. When Jesus came, scandalously healing on the Sabbath, he was denounced.[1] No man of God worked when God had clearly forbidden it.

Jesus didn't skirt these tricky Sabbath questions; he apparently forced them. Though the lame man in today's reading had not walked for thirty-eight years, though it would have been nothing for Jesus to delay his healing one more day, he chose a Sabbath Saturday to perform the miracle. It was a means of laying claim to divine prerogative and identity: "My Father is working until now, and I am working." In the first century, Jewish theologians and philosophers worked themselves into knots trying to understand the work that God did and didn't do on the Sabbath. Many agreed that it was no violation of the Sabbath for God to give life (as babies continue to be born on the Sabbath) and for God to judge (as people continue to die on the Sabbath). In this story, Jesus aligns himself with both of these divine activities.

Jesus's claim to divinity is one of great consequence—a claim for which people will accuse him of blasphemy and which will eventually cost him his life. But as John does not hesitate to affirm, there is only one God in human flesh, and it's Jesus Christ, born in a remote corner of the Roman Empire in the first century. There is one voice alone that raises the dead and calls them to give him account for their lives. Jesus is not simply a divine healer, a man endowed with fantastical powers. He is God.

Whatever our religious (or irreligious) background, like the Jewish leaders, we bring a particular set of conceptions to what God is like and how we can expect him to act. This is why the healing of the lame man by the pool of Bethesda begs a closer look for its surprises. This miracle is accompanied by no fanfare, no spectacle, no loud, public pronouncements that God has come in the flesh. Instead, after Jesus makes this man's shriveled legs strong, he slips back into the crowd, determined to stay anonymous. The lame man hasn't even caught Jesus's name!

Surely this is *not* how God does public relations.

Jesus's furtive movements in this story aren't the only surprise. It's also worth noting that Jesus first asks the man, "Do you want to be healed?" before performing the miracle. It's not that this man's faith or cooperation is needed to shore up something lacking in Jesus's power, but the question Jesus asks underlines a quality of God's love and power: it is never coercive. Being God, Jesus would surely be entitled to do whatever he wants whenever he wants. But Jesus is no gun-slinging God. In fact, as the Reformer Martin Luther wrote back in the sixteenth century, Jesus demonstrates God's preference for "left-handed power," which is to say weak power.[2] He did not arrive on the first-century scene and demand, under penalty of death, that people bow, giving the honor due him as God. He chose a different means of saving the world—even death on a cross.

In arranging the clues of this great mystery story, John has rallied a number of witnesses for his Gospel account. He cites the testimony of John the Baptist, "a burning and shining lamp" who spoke of Jesus, the greater Light. He recalls the thundering voice of God the Father at the baptism of Jesus, pronouncing that Jesus was in fact God's Son.[3] The works of Jesus also testified to his divine identity as the Christ, the Son of God. Yet as John points out, perhaps the greatest witness—at least the one mattering most to this group of biblical scholars whom Jesus addresses in this passage—was the Hebrew Scriptures. As John explains, when Moses spoke, out of his mouth tumbled the very words of Jesus. Deuteronomy, then, is not just a collection of Moses's sermons—but also of Jesus's.

Deuteronomy pronounced both blessing and curse over the people of God: blessing for obedience, curse for disobedience. *Live*, Moses entreated the people of Israel! In the very same way, life is to be found in Jesus's words—death in refusing them (v. 40).

It's another reminder that faith makes a habit of heeding the words—and Word—of God.

For Reflection/Discussion

In what ways does Jesus confirm your expectations of what God is like? In what ways does Jesus challenge your expectations?

PREMI SURESH

"I started to realize how
the gospel changes everything."

Premi Suresh grew up in an observant Catholic family. "If we were on vacation, we went to church. We could not miss church." Premi did all the sacraments and regularly volunteered at the church as an altar server, a reader at Mass, and a Sunday school teacher. "Looking back, it felt like something you did on Sunday. It didn't apply to the rest of the week."

After high school, Premi was accepted into a six-year BS/MD program. In college, she stopped attending church. "I realized I was doing all those things because my family was doing them, but I didn't personally feel that I needed to do it." Two years into the program, Premi opted for a semester study abroad in Switzerland where she traveled with a classmate. They attended Mass at Notre Dame in Paris as well as Mass at the Vatican; they even had the chance to see the Pope. "But I was very troubled at that time. We had toured Dachau, one of the concentration camps. I knew the Pope and the Catholic church basically said nothing during the Holocaust. Where were they?"

When Premi returned to campus, an acquaintance asked to set her up on a blind date, and she soon fell in love with the man who would become her husband. When Premi and Preetham decided to get married, they faced challenges in planning their ceremony in the Catholic church. "His family couldn't take communion [because they weren't Catholic]. So we didn't have communion, but that was upsetting to my family. I kept thinking, 'This is so stupid. It's causing all this unnecessary conflict when everything's supposed to be so happy.'"

After the wedding, Premi and Preetham moved to San Francisco for their medical residencies and, at the suggestion of Preetham's mom, began attending a Presbyterian church. Their involvement, however, ended after the Sunday morning service each week. When Premi's sister asked the couple to become the godparents of her baby, she indicated they'd need a letter from their church, attesting their attendance. Reluctantly, Premi called the church office, sheepish to admit that she couldn't name any members of the church and didn't belong to a small group. "Well, you get checks from us," she hesitatingly offered. The church agreed to write the letter on the condition that the couple join a small group, which they did. Although they liked the leaders of the group, who made efforts to understand their faith questions, Premi and Preetham never felt entirely comfortable in the setting, especially when it came time for sharing prayer requests. Crediting her successes to her own efforts, Premi was tempted to think, *You really just don't make good decisions with your life* when others shared their requests.

After their medical residencies, Premi and Preetham moved to San Diego. It took them a couple of years of "floating around" to commit to a church. At the same time, the couple began trying to have a baby, and for the first time in Premi's life, she planned for something that didn't happen. "We bought a five-bedroom house, but there were no kids [to fill the bedrooms]." Again, Preetham's mom encouraged them to settle into a church. She suggested a

Presbyterian church within walking distance, which they began regularly attending.

"As I rewind the journey, I can see signposts along the way, and they fall into three different areas. The first is that of unmet expectations. Then there's the road of recognizing my depravity. The final path was [confronting] the truth of the gospel." For four years, Premi and Preetham tried to have a baby but to no avail. "I remember our pastor and his wife coming over for dinner one night. Paul asked me very kindly, 'Is Jesus enough? I know you want this baby, but if this baby is not going to be a part of God's plan, is Jesus enough?'" Premi admitted that she didn't understand the question. "How could Jesus be enough? What does that even mean?"

That dinner conversation took place in July 2012, during the year that Premi had committed to reading through the Bible chronologically. (She'd wanted to shore up what seemed to be her deficient knowledge of this "fundamental text.") She also began to pray more that year, although mostly for a baby. "I felt guilty about that." Still, in December, just as she was finishing the reading plan, Premi became pregnant with their daughter, Simran, which means "gift from God." "I was reveling in my pregnancy, so happy, so excited. But I promptly forgot about God. I got what I wanted."

This new baby, however, did not fulfill all the longings Premi thought she would. "Again, unmet expectations. I have this baby, the one thing I wanted, after praying for four years, and then I realize, *Gosh, this is hard.*" Premi had returned to her work as a pediatrician, and as she tried to juggle the demands of pumping her breast milk and seeing patients, she grew more and more resentful about the disproportionate burdens she seemed to be shouldering when compared to her husband. She tried consoling herself that things would get better—"when the baby is sleeping through the night"—but she distinctly remembered a sermon she'd heard during that season. "Our pastor said, 'If you're hoping that the next stage of life will bring you contentment, whatever it is you're waiting for, it's not going to bring contentment either."

In addition to facing unmet expectations, Premi also had to acknowledge that she wasn't the mother she had envisioned herself being. "I'd always thought, *I'm a pretty good person. I don't need religion because I'm pretty generous.*" She'd pictured herself being a "sweet, patient, and loving" mother. In reality, she had to admit that she was far more often "angry, irritable, and frustrated. . . . I'd try to make excuses," Premi said, but she knew these habits of character weren't functions of sleep deprivation. They were chronic issues, and they were also affecting her marriage.

At the time, a friend from church recommended a book, which Premi read and immediately tried to forget. "The book was very frank. In no uncertain terms, it said, 'You are the problem.'" Though reluctantly, Premi began to admit this truth about herself: "I'd been holding people around me to a standard of perfection to fulfill my need for perfect love, which we all have. But that need can only be fulfilled by the Creator, not by people."

After the American presidential election in 2016, Premi was heartbroken and angry. "I was hearing that it was White evangelicals, that it was the Christian vote that elected Trump." She began to question whether she was even a Christian, and for a number of months, she immersed herself in Ted Talks, self-help books, and mindfulness techniques. But she also began listening to old sermons from her church, including a series on the book of Ecclesiastes. "Those sermons tied to the whole contentment theme. It was a pivotal book for me. [It said] there is no contentment or fulfillment under the sun. You can pursue achievement, pleasure, all these things, but you'll still be left with vapor. The only way to find contentment is through God." Influenced by a Ted Talk on habits, Premi abandoned Facebook for thirty days and took up reading the New Testament instead. "At the end of those thirty days, I started to realize how the gospel changes everything."

"When we first began attending [Redeemer Presbyterian San Diego] and our pastor gave the message, I noticed that it always ended with Jesus. He would say, 'When this truth takes hold, it will change everything. The gospel changes everything.' I'd hear that and think, *But I've known the gospel my whole life, and it hasn't changed anything*." However, after reading the New Testament and teachings such as "Whoever tries to save his life will lose it, and whoever loses his life for me will find life," Premi finally began to understand what her pastor meant. She realized that to embrace faith in Jesus, "There's no way you can keep living your same life."

Premi was about to turn forty when she attended her church's women's retreat and began, in earnest, to follow Jesus. "It seems symbolic. For forty years, I was lost. Maybe this next chapter can be spent walking with God."

"Drawing near to God and knowing that God provides me with that perfect love so that I can learn to love others—this is how life is meant to be lived."

Premi Suresh is a newfound follower of Jesus, a wife, a mother of two, and a pediatrician in San Diego.

DAY 26

Read John 6:1–71 (Focus: vv. 52–59)

Key Verse: "I am the bread of life; whoever comes to me shall not hunger, and whoever believes in me shall never thirst." (*v. 35*)

God's Gift of Bread

Our friends arrived for dinner before I'd had the chance to shape the biscuit dough and cut the rounds. They watched as I floured the counter and twisted the mason jar, cutting perfect rounds and sliding them onto a baking sheet. As we watched the biscuits rise in the oven, Paul told me excitedly about a prototype for a new small appliance that his company had developed. It had all the convenience of a pod coffee maker—except that each pod held an individually-sized portion of bread dough. But as I tried explaining to him, half the reason for making bread is the pleasure of working the dough.

Even more miraculous than hot rolls at the press of a button was Jesus's act of feeding a teeming crowd from a little boy's lunchbox.[1] Aside from Jesus's resurrection, this is the only miracle that all four Gospel writers record, lending it unique prominence among the other accounts of Jesus's healings and exorcisms. Still, this stunning miracle, as we are learning to expect, is not the road paved to power. Instead, after Jesus has sent the hungry crowds away full and his disciples have seen him walking on water, the crowds thin out. There is attrition in the ranks of the disciples. The crowds have wanted Jesus to take power in a certain way and for certain political purposes, but Jesus has shown no interest in either their means or ends. It's as if he's the host of a political convention, and just as the crowd's enthusiasm swells to a feverish pitch, he's dampened the mood by asking for the lights to be dimmed and the music to be turned off.

It's not that Jesus simply favors being an iconoclast. In the Gospel of John, we see Jesus against the backdrop of Jewish religious traditions: his sojourns to Jerusalem for the prescribed pilgrimage feasts, his regular attendance at the synagogue for worship. Though he is accused of having violated the Sabbath, he is a model Jew, well-versed in the Hebrew Scriptures and competent to teach them. In fact, in John, Jesus is portrayed as a Moses figure. Just as we knew Moses to be a man of the mountain, disappearing into the cloud of God's presence, Jesus too climbs heights both to teach his disciples and to seek solitude.

For all their similarities, however, it's clear that Jesus is greater than Moses. The two greatest signs and wonders that God ever performed through Moses in the wilderness were the parting of the Red Sea and feeding the multitudes with manna. But Moses, of course, had not produced the manna himself, only trusted that God would provide it as promised. And he had not parted the raging waters of the Red Sea himself, only stood on its banks with his staff upraised. Jesus's power, however, is far greater. He is the living water and the bread of life.

John is calling for a transfer of allegiance here. All the loyalty the people of Israel once pledged to Moses (if inconsistently, at best) was now meant to be pledged to Jesus. All the hope they'd invested in the Torah and the "work" of keeping its words was to be invested in Jesus, believing that he was the Word, the Christ, the Son of God.

In John's Gospel, Jesus has already twice used for himself the name by which God introduced himself when Moses met him in the mystery of a burning bush.[2] When Moses had asked God's name, God had answered, "I AM": *Yahweh* in the Hebrew, *ego eimi* in the Greek. Strikingly, it's this very phrase—*ego eimi*—that Jesus used in answering the Samaritan woman when she spoke of the coming Messiah. "He will tell us all things," she had said. *I AM*, Jesus had answered. Jesus also used this phrase when consoling the disciples, who were frightened by his figure walking on a storm-tossed sea: *I AM*.[3]

Jesus is God. He is also the *true Israel*—the perfectly obedient Son of God that Israel could never be. To emphasize this point, we might first note John's deliberate inclusion—twice—of Jesus's act of giving thanks for the bread. It seems like such a small detail, and some would simply take it as a reminder to bow our heads at the dinner table. But certainly more is suggested here. It's not hard to remember how ungrateful Israel was in receiving God's gift of bread in the wilderness. They were constantly grumbling about the menu. Jesus, by contrast, received God's simple fare with thanksgiving.

In John 4, we learned that Jesus is the living water; in today's reading, we learned that Jesus is the living bread. In both stories, these offers of Jesus to quench thirst and sate stomachs are greedily received. "Sir, give me this water!" "Sir, give us this bread!" As human beings, we know what it is to be parched and hungry. And we know this not simply in a physical sense but also in a spiritual one. We know what it's like to invest our hopes in having a good job, a good marriage, the next vacation, a bigger house, healthy children, a growing retirement account. To be sure, all these good things deliver a certain amount of satisfaction and a degree of happiness. But there is one terrible cruelty in everything this world has to offer: it never lasts. Health fails; children leave; marriages end; money dries up. Every version of the good life—whether career achievement, financial stability, domestic happiness—leaks. Nothing is strong enough, reliable enough, or lasting enough to support our deepest longings and hopes.

Except Jesus: this bread and water of endless supply.

But there's a catch to this offer. It's not the catch of contract exclusions, written in fine print. It's this: to have the living bread and the living water, one will have to receive what God did in the death of Jesus. One will have to partake of and participate in the broken body and shed blood of Christ.

The meaning of this cryptic command will only become clear as the final events of Jesus's life unfold.

For Reflection/Discussion

When have you felt your "hunger" and "thirst" most acutely? What might it look like for you to actively trust that Jesus is the only one who can satisfy your deepest desires?

DAY 27

Read John 7:1–8:59 (Focus: 7:37–44)

Key Verse: "If you abide in my word, you are truly my disciples." (8:31)

Identity Verification

Whenever I make a new Canadian acquaintance, it's not long before they halt the conversation to ask, "Wait—are you American?" Most would say my nasal vowels give me away. Even in our age of global mobility, when so many of us find ourselves far from home, our places of origin have the potential for conveying credibility or communicating suspicion. When I traveled to Alabama recently to speak at a church, I tried making overtures, despite my Yankee accent: "I lived six years of my childhood in Tennessee. I know the best flour for making biscuits!"

Every Gospel account begins with a particular emphasis on Jesus's origins. Unlike John, who insists on Jesus's eternality, Matthew, Mark, and Luke emphasize Jesus's family lineage and his birthplace. These details come to divide the crowds in John 7.

The crowds have learned from the prophets that the Messiah, the one sent by God and anointed for his special purposes, will be born in Bethlehem into the royal family of David, Israel's second king.[1] But if Jesus is from Nazareth, isn't this proof that he's *not* the one they've been expecting? Rather than clear the confusion and recount Joseph and Mary's trek to Bethlehem in the late stages of her pregnancy for the Roman census,[2] Jesus remains somewhat cryptic: "You are from below; I am from above." Further, in chapter 8, he tells the crowd that it is less the *beginning* of his story that will authenticate that he is the Christ, the Son of God—and more the *end*. "When you have lifted up the Son of Man, then you will know that I am he, and that I do nothing on my own authority, but speak just as the Father taught me." The cross of Jesus, even more than the cradle of Jesus, will confirm his identity.

The question of identity is at the center of all four of the Gospels. Who is Jesus? Unlike Deuteronomy, the Gospel of John is the exposé of a man, not simply a message. In John's Gospel, we're not merely meeting Jesus as a wise teacher. He's no self-help author or life coach, offering tips and tricks to help us achieve career success, family happiness, and inner well-being. Nor are we meeting him, in John's account, as humanity's own genie in a bottle, conjuring hocus-pocus power and creating spectacle in his wake.

Jesus brings a message far more divisive than "your best life now." He identifies humanity's greatest problem as sin, even "slavery" to sin. Though we tend to think about sin in terms of God's nitpicky moral standards, in the Gospel of John, sin often means the rejection of Jesus. Sin is humanity's inhospitality to the Word of God. Sin is our preference for autonomy, our presumption of self-righteousness. Sin may come in the form of mild disinterest or venomous antipathy, but however it comes, sin keeps God at arm's length. *Out of our business.*

In these two chapters, Jesus has traveled back to Jerusalem for the Feast of Booths, the most beloved and festive of the three Jewish pilgrim feasts.[3] It's by no means accidental that he speaks again of water and light, for these two symbols were central in the celebration of this festival. Each day of the weeklong holiday, the priests processed to the southern border of Jerusalem, filled a golden pitcher with water at the Pool of Siloam, and returned to the temple. As the crowds thronged around them, singing from the words of the prophet Isaiah—"With joy you will draw water from the wells of salvation"[4]—the priest poured the water over the altar. The rite was meant as a visual picture of Israel's future hope, when water would flow from the eternal temple, becoming a great river to nourish the world.[5] When Jesus stood to preach that he was "the light of the world," he was standing in the treasury, or The Court of Women. During this same holiday, sixteen large bowls, reached only by ladders, were filled with oil and lit, illumining all of Jerusalem.

During the Feast of Booths, as the people remembered the scarcities of the wilderness and God's provision, Jesus was saying: I was there! I was the bread for your hunger, the water for your thirst, the light for your darkness. I am the greater Moses—and an even greater sign and wonder than the manna, the water from the rock, and the towering cloud of light that guided you on every moonless night. Just as Moses promised blessing for those who obeyed the words of God, I, too, hold out life to those who believe and follow me. "If you abide in my word, you are truly my disciples, and you will know the truth, and the truth will set you free."

In his book *Mere Christianity*, C. S. Lewis memorably said that Jesus's words either prove him to be a liar, lunatic, or Lord.[6] In weighing Jesus's words, we might return to the question of the trustworthiness of John's account of this man's words as well as this man's life. This was the first line of inquiry that *Chicago Tribune* reporter Lee Strobel pursued years ago after his wife had become a follower of Jesus. What he discovered (and recorded in his bestselling book *The Case for Christ*) was overwhelming evidence in favor of the historical reliability of the four Gospels. Compared to the Greek *Iliad*, for which there are only 650 manuscripts in existence today, all of them 800 years removed from the time of Homer's writing, the Bible has an astonishing 5,000 (partial) manuscripts, the earliest dating from AD 200. In fact, the oldest fragment of the Bible in existence is from John 18, and scholars date it at AD 100–150. The multiplicity of manuscripts and the early dating of the writings of Matthew, Mark, Luke, and John bolster the case that we can trust that these accounts have come to us from within the eyewitnesses' generation.

Moreover, we see evidence in today's reading of the vested interest Christians have had in re-creating the original monographs of the Bible in our English translations. In the marginal notes from today's reading, many of us discover that John 7:53–8:11 wasn't included in the earliest manuscripts of John. Although most scholars agree that this incident with Jesus exonerating the adulterous woman did in fact happen and was likely transmitted in the oral record, it's not original to John, which is why it has been omitted.

In the crowds as well as in Jesus's own family, some believed—and some doubted. Some remained curious—and some turned murderous. Jesus was then—and continues now to be—a polarizing figure. No one can reserve judgment about the identity of Jesus and safely straddle the fence.

Everyone must answer this question: Who is Jesus?

For Reflection/Discussion

Who are you most like in the crowd: the curious, the doubting, the believing, or the angry? What reasons do you have for trusting Jesus? For mistrusting him?

DAY 28

Read John 9:1–41 (Focus: vv. 35–41)

Key Verse: "If you were blind, you would have no guilt; but now that you say, 'We see,' your guilt remains." (v. 41)

The Dawning of Day

Living in a large city, I encounter homeless people nearly every day. In fact, many are neighbors whom I'm guaranteed to bump into regularly on the sidewalk or at the local Tim Horton's. One man is tall and lean, his white hair wild and wiry, his beard long. No matter the weather, he is always dressed in a tattered sport coat, which lends him an absentminded, professorial air. Another is often heard muttering to himself, as if holding animated conversation with an invisible friend. His nervous tics calm when he lights a bummed cigarette. A third neighbor—a woman—stands at the swinging door of the local convenience store with two large suitcases beside her, shaking the coins in a coffee cup. I imagine she's pressed to board the bus at the corner.

Embarrassingly, I've never had a sustained conversation with any of these neighbors. My negligence makes me think of the people in today's story, these "neighbors" who come to the temple daily, paying such scant attention to the blind beggar at the gates that when they're asked to identify him, they can't be sure of the features of his face and the quality of his voice. This beggar has been invisible to them as they've made sure not to be late for church.

It is no small irony that Jesus's disciples turn the begging man into a theological object lesson. They don't first look to alleviate his suffering. Instead, they look to parse its meaning. Who had sinned that he should suffer blindness from birth?

The disciples assumed the logic of divine retribution: God blessed the good and cursed the wicked. Perhaps they were thinking of Deuteronomy 28, when the twelve tribes of Israel were commanded to call out the blessings and the curses from the summits of Mount Ebal and Mount Gerizim.[1] Six of the tribes proclaimed obedience as a protection for God's people. Six warned that disobedience would lead to swift disaster. Jesus himself had also made a similar connection—between sin and sickness—when warning the healed paralytic in John 5.

But Jesus isn't as quick here as his disciples to systematize a theology of suffering. His concern in this story is less for the theoretical—and more for the human. He wants to heal this man. While we aren't privy to the different kinds of healing accounts offered in the Gospels of Matthew, Mark, and Luke, which picture Jesus thronged by the diseased and the demon-possessed, in John, we're witness to Jesus's sustained one-on-one encounters with the sick.

In John's Gospel, Jesus the healer is also Jesus the Creator. As John 9 opens, the Festival of Tabernacles is at its close. From ancient historians we know that the Feast, prescribed as a seven-day festival in the Scriptures, had lengthened into an eight-day celebration by the time of Jesus. According to one writer,[2] on that eighth day, the cycle of Torah readings began anew in Genesis 1: "In the beginning, God created the heavens and the earth. . . . And God said, 'Let there be light.'"

If these are indeed the words ringing in the ears of those gathered, it seems John intends to amplify those echoes of the Genesis creation narrative in his account. Jesus is the light—and he is also the one who calls light into being; he is the Creator—and he is also the re-creator. He makes blind men see. As God had stooped to form Adam from the dust of the earth, breathing into his inert form the breath of life, so too Jesus stoops to scoop dirt, making a mud paste with his saliva. In a very real sense, this blind man is a kind of Adam figure, and it's the dawning of a new day.

At the very beginning when God brought the world into being, it was, in God's own words, "very good." Only when humanity rebelled against God was the world cursed by sin and sentenced to death. But when Jesus steps into time, he comes to reverse sin's curse. This grand drama is enacted here in the story of one blind beggar. Not only is he healed from physical blindness, but he is also healed from spiritual blindness. For at the end of the account, the beggar has come to see Christ with unhindered clarity: as more than the man called Jesus, as more than a prophet, but as Lord—the one worthy to be worshiped as God alone deserves.

The story relayed in John 9 became a very important story for the teaching of the early Christian church, a story commonly depicted in early catacomb art.[3] In fact, the healing of the blind man was used in examinations for baptismal candidates as the church grew.[4] People came to this text with the assumption that it served as a template for understanding the nature of faith. Every person had to admit his or her blindness in order to receive the healing only Christ can perform.

Spiritual blindness is a congenital disease afflicting every human being. It doesn't matter our education, our cultural savvy, our progressive politics, our religious upbringing, our exemplary moral record. We are all blind, and sin makes it impossible to see our need for God. Our morally crooked impulse is to let ourselves off the hook, to lay blame at anyone's feet but our own.

The only way we can come to Jesus is by admitting our moral indebtedness—and that we can't heal our own blindness.

Habits of humility pave the road to faith.

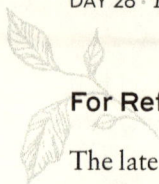

For Reflection/Discussion

The late British theologian Lesslie Newbigin wrote, "The distinction is not between those who are blind and those who see; it is between those who know they are blind and those who claim they can see."[5] What do you make of the claim that every human being is spiritually blind? Is this something that you "see" about yourself?

DAY 29

Read John 10:1–42 (Focus: vv. 14–18)

Key Verses: "I lay down my life that I may take it up again. No one takes it from me." (vv. 17–18)

Born to Be Free

Years ago, at the wedding of close friends, the service opened with congregational singing. My own heart limped along with the music. It wasn't that I was suffering a crisis of faith, but on this particular day, I could not rouse myself to any real enthusiasm. Then the musicians began to play a worship song based on the Apostles' Creed, reciting some of the earliest affirmations of Christian faith: "I believe in God the Father; I believe in Christ the Son; I believe in the Holy Spirit, our God is three in one." It's then that I began to cry, if only for the simple reason that I was not required to *feel* any certain way about God. I had only to attest to his reality.

John 10 makes me recall that moment. Like the singing or reciting of the Apostles' Creed, there is something in Jesus's words here that relieves us of the pressure to make faith a subjective experience, something to be confirmed or denied by our own feelings. Instead, Christian faith is centered on the person and work of Jesus Christ—this "door" and this "shepherd." Although the Christian might feel his own faith to be fraying at the edges, although the skeptic may fear that doubt itself excludes him from belonging to God, Christian faith has a far more fixed and stable point.

Christian faith isn't authenticated by our emotional experience of it but by its object, Jesus Christ.

This is, of course, what's anathema about the gospel in a pluralist world. Jesus doesn't say, *I'm one of many doors* or *I'm one of many shepherds*. He narrows infinite possibilities of faith into the tiniest stricture of a definite article: *the*. God has only one means of entrance into the good life, both here and hereafter. It's Jesus.

The earliest apostles and the early church fathers preached this radically exclusive message—and usually suffered for it. Similarly today, for those who hold to the idea that salvation is found in Jesus alone, they are accused of bigotry. But though we might wish it were true that every religion charted a reliable path to God, that's not the testimony of John's Gospel, nor of the rest of the New Testament.

When Jesus speaks of his identity as the "good shepherd," he's connecting to very old ideas in Jewish Scripture of God as Israel's shepherd.[1] Since the time of Moses, God had appointed human shepherds to lead in his stead.[2] God called Israel's second king from the sheepfolds, setting the youngest shepherd son of Jesse on the throne.[3] Many centuries later, after both the northern and southern kingdoms of Israel were taken into exile, the prophet Isaiah wrote about the coming of another servant of God, from the throne of David, who would allow himself to be led to the slaughter.[4] That shepherd would act from self-sacrificing love for the sake of his sheep. Unlike the false shepherds that the prophet Ezekiel described, who did not tend to the sick and the injured and the strayed, the good shepherd would throw his own body into the path of danger in order to save his sheep.[5]

Jesus is that Good Shepherd, and his act of self-sacrifice is his surrender to the cross. As we've seen previously, the story of John's Gospel is moving steadily uphill to Golgotha where Jesus, the Good Shepherd, will lay down his life for the sheep. This isn't to say that the story of Jesus is primarily a story of noble martyrdom, as if Jesus is only to be admired and imitated for his courage or righteous principles. His life is not taken from him but willingly given. The Father has loved the world so much that he has given his Son; the Son has loved the sheep so much that he will give his life. And while the cross could seem like the ultimate absurdity, even in this, God is stubbornly pursuing his ends of love.

Love, not cruelty or chance, is the beating heart of God's universe.

What's at work in Jesus is a divine paradox: both his freedom and his obedience. In our contemporary constructs, we think of freedom as the absence of constraints. We are free insofar as we can do exactly as we please. But while it was Jesus's privilege to do exactly as he willed, even to avoid the cruel torture of the cross, Jesus was also bound to the obligations of his own love, a love that could never abandon the sheep.

We are never more free—and more bound—than when we apprentice ourselves to Jesus. He is the path to abundant life.

For Reflection/Discussion

What is illuminated about the life of faith in Jesus when it's understood as a dynamic between shepherd and sheep? Would you say that you can recognize the voice of Jesus?

DAY 30

Read John 11:1–57 (Focus: vv. 25–27)

Key Verse: "I am the resurrection and the life. Whoever believes in me, though he die, yet shall he live." (*v.* 25)

Dead Man Walking

I still have her name in my contacts, still have saved messages from her on my phone. We didn't keep in close touch after I moved to Toronto, although a year before her cancer diagnosis, we had tried to get together when she was flying through Canada for work. When I did manage to see her one final time on a visit to Chicago, she was doing laps around the oncology ward, pushing her IV pole. Several months later, she was dead.

I think about death a lot. My father died at forty-nine, my brother at twenty-five. I think about death when I'm crossing bridges and crossing streets. I hold my children back when we stand at busy street corners, averting the sudden catastrophe of a car losing control. They roll their eyes, and I try laughing too. But I know how life can be wrenched from any of us in an instant.

Arriving at John 11, we see Jesus's reaction to death. Jesus is not coolly aloof on the occasion of the death of his friend Lazarus. Instead, he is wrenched, angry, and deeply troubled. Gratefully, we don't find Jesus sermonizing at the entrance of the sealed tomb, serving up platitudes to the grieving crowd. Instead, we find the Word of God, older than time itself, weeping. Most importantly, at the graveside of Lazarus, we discover Jesus's power over death.

Four days after Lazarus's burial, when his soul would have been long gone, Jesus speaks these simple, authoritative words: "Lazarus, come out."[1]

In John's Gospel, the raising of Lazarus brings to completion the witness of the seven signs the Evangelist has carefully recorded: Jesus has turned water into wine, healed a royal official's son, fed a crowd of five thousand, walked on water, made a lame man walk, made a blind man see, and now raised a dead man alive. In John's account, each of these extraordinary events are "signs," disclosing the reality that God had indeed moved into the neighborhood. They are signs of God's glory—and signs of God's goodness.[2]

As Jesus showers the favor of God in these tangible ways, it becomes clear that God has not given up on his covenant promises to Israel, despite their unfaithfulness to him. Centuries before Christ, after the nation of Israel had gone into exile, Isaiah prophesied that God would send his anointed servant to reverse the many curses of sin, and these promises were the text of Jesus's first sermon in Nazareth: "The Spirit of the Lord is upon me, because he has anointed me to proclaim good news to the poor. He has sent me to proclaim liberty to the captives and recovering of sight to the blind, to set at liberty those who are oppressed, to proclaim the year of the Lord's favor."[3] In Jesus, the blessings of God, spoken so long ago to the people of Israel at the edge of the promised land, were coming true.[4]

These signs seem like incontrovertible evidence that Jesus is who he says he is. The eyewitnesses, however, remain divided. Some believe—but some report the raising of Lazarus to the Pharisees, as if reporting a crime. Even the disciples' belief has a quality of gradual awakening, dawning in the way that the sun rises. After receiving the message of Lazarus's illness, Jesus explains his delay in going to his friend as the means for growing the disciples' faith: he wants them to "believe." Martha too sees her own faith grow and expand through the story. She's surely trusted Jesus to heal her brother, but even after Jesus's pronouncement of his identity—"I am the resurrection and the life"—she hasn't absorbed the truth as anything more than metaphor. When Jesus calls for the removal of the stone from the tomb's entrance, she cautions him that her brother will stink. Martha too must be invited into a greater "seeing" and "believing."

The raising of Lazarus commends to us both Jesus's humanity and Jesus's divinity. Jesus is *God* in the flesh, and he has the power to raise the dead. But Jesus is also God *in the flesh*, revealing what it means to be truly human. As the true human, Jesus loved so deeply as to feel the knife blade of grief when his close friend died. Three times we're reminded of how much Jesus loved Lazarus and his two sisters, and such details help us to imagine Jesus, not as some stoic superhuman but as someone like us, who knew the experiences of both love and loss.

Just as we see Jesus's humanity in this story, we also see faith as a deeply human venture—as something dynamic rather than static. The great leader of the Protestant Reformation, Martin Luther, said that "he who *is* a Christian is no Christian."[5] In other words, faith in Jesus is not a once-and-done proposition. It is not only decided once; it is decided daily. It is not only past; it is also continuously present. It is both a conversion—and also a habit. We choose belief every day, choosing to trust that Jesus is the Good Shepherd and that we can trust his voice.

It is, of course, striking that we have no firsthand account from Lazarus after he's unbound from his graveclothes. Although we'll see him again in John 12, we'll never hear him recount his experience of death in his own words. His silence in the text speaks to the essential meaning of the event: it's not, in fact, about Lazarus at all. His death and resurrection are meant to foreshadow another death and another resurrection: a resurrection requiring no human hands to roll away the stone and unbind the graveclothes. Jesus's loud cry, "Lazarus, come out!" reminds us of the loud cry that

Luke recorded in his account of the crucifixion, when Jesus, "calling out with a loud voice said, 'Father, into your hands I commit my spirit.' And having said this, he breathed his last."[6]

In the recorded words of the high priest, Caiaphas, we know the meaning we're intended to find in the last of the seven signs. As one man, Jesus will die for the people of God. And it will indeed be "better" for us.

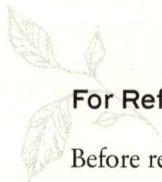

For Reflection/Discussion

Before reading this passage, how might you have imagined Jesus responding to the death of a friend? Does Jesus's promise of resurrection and eternal life feel like a pie-in-the-sky hope—or something to be trusted as true?

KIM DEMCHUK

"God, if you're real, heal me."

Kim Demchuk described her household growing up as "spiritual." Her parents had divorced when she was two, and her mother took her and her two siblings to a traditional United Church [of Canada] on Sunday mornings. "It looked good for us to go to church. It was the socially acceptable thing to do." Kim also fondly recalled a friendship she built with a local pastor who lived near her elementary school and invited her to Bible club. He even paid for her to attend a summer Bible camp. "I can see how God put certain people in my life, even when I was a child."

If Sunday mornings found Kim and her family at church, respectably dressed and decently behaved, behind closed doors, their home life was characterized by chaos and violence. Much of her mom's attention was devoted to her siblings, both diagnosed with mental disorders. Because Kim's mother suffered from bipolar disorder and the stress of caring for her high-needs children, her vulnerabilities led her to become increasingly violent. "She's not the same person today," Kim defended before recollecting how she'd often watched her siblings getting beaten growing up.

For a number of years, Kim worked desperately to gain her mother's attention by trying to attain perfection in a number of different areas: in school, in athletic competition, in musical performance. "It didn't matter." As Kim's mother told her many years later, "I didn't think I had to [be there for you] because you were okay." When Kim finally tired of trying to earn her mother's affection, she let her mom "have it." That violent confrontation was a turning point, both in their relationship and in Kim's life. Kim attempted suicide and was hospitalized. When her mother visited the psych ward, she physically attacked Kim again, prompting Kim to move in with her father.

Until this point, Kim's father had never been a regular part of her life. "He was facing his own demons," Kim explained, referring to his gambling addiction and alcoholism as reasons for his absence. "Then, all of a sudden, there's this fourteen-year-old girl that you barely know, and she gets dropped off at your doorstep. And now, you have to deal with all of this garbage." Soon, Kim was involved with drugs and gangs, looking to soothe the pain of her broken childhood and the violence she'd witnessed. "I remember walking into four-lane traffic right in front of my high school, hoping that someone would hit me. When there's constant pain, you just want it to end."

After a couple of years of living with her father and stepmother, another household marked by tumult and physical abuse, she moved out and at the age of sixteen, effectively became homeless. "I was couch surfing for the most part, just moving from place to place to place." Eventually, she met a girl at a party who invited her to move into her apartment, which was located in Kim's hometown where her mother still lived. That's where Kim met her future husband, Chad. Several months later she moved in with him.

Despite being raised in a Christian family, Chad's lifestyle was hardly distinguishable from Kim's. Although he claimed to believe in Jesus, even to love him, "he was partying, he was having a good old time." When a Pentecostal preacher came into town to hold healing services, Chad's mother invited them both to attend. "She knew that I suffered a lot from a physical condition." When Kim was six years old, her family's car had been hit by a drunk driver, and the force of the impact crushed Kim's bowels and bladder. Although surgery had repaired much of the damage, Kim still suffered bouts of occasional swelling. "I would look like I was eight months pregnant," she described. Knowing this, Chad's mother had simply said to Kim, "You should come," then let the prospect of healing linger between them. "Because what if?"

"There was a piece of hope that I wanted God to be real more than anything in the world, that I did not want him to be pain." She tested God, as she remembered it, before arriving the night of the healing service. "Who am I to test God?" But Kim recalled praying a very simple prayer with the tiniest mustard seed of faith. "All I said was: 'God, if you're real, heal me.'"

On the night of the healing service, Peter Youngren, a Canadian Christian evangelist, began speaking as if having a very particular vision of someone in the room. "I feel like there is a young lady here who has suffered in her bowels and in her bladder," he announced. "You swell, and there is this knotty pain that you experience." Kim elbowed Chad in astonishment: "There is someone here with the exact same thing as me!" When no one stood, Youngren continued. "I'm going to wait for you," he said, speaking of this young woman and her swollen abdomen. "God wants to heal you. You asked God to show up, and he's showing up." At this point, Chad elbowed Kim in the ribs. "He's talking about you!"

"I was completely petrified. I had absolutely no experience with this kind of thing." As she walked toward the front, her entire body was shaking as the crowd watched. "I have all these strangers looking at me. I'm a nobody—yet God calls me up?" When she reached the front, Youngren reached out his hand and scarcely grazed Kim's forehead. She immediately fell to the ground. "All I feel is this heat from my head going all the way down." Petrified, crying, and unable to get up, Kim turned over to army crawl back to her seat. She was gently stopped by an older woman from the congregation, who came to put her hand on her back. "Honey, just stay. Let the Holy Spirit do what the Holy Spirit needs to do."

Although she didn't know it at the time, Kim was instantly healed. What she did understand, however, was the pursuing, self-sacrificing love of God expressed through Christ—that he'd died for her. She remembered praying, "Lord, I'm a nobody. You picked me, somebody who wanted to be loved so badly but decided to go the opposite way. You're not the God of pain. You're the God of love."

Kimberly Demchuk has been married to Chad for over twenty-five years, and they have two children, Brooke and Michael. They all proudly live in Leduc, Alberta, and have attended Daystar Church for over nineteen years.

DAY 31

Read John 12:1–50 (Focus: vv. 27–32)

Key Verse: "For I have not spoken on my own authority, but the Father who sent me has himself given me a commandment—what to say and what to speak." (*v. 49*)

Hail to the Chief

Every time I travel to the States, I hear the divided ways people talk about the current president, Donald Trump. (It's early 2020 as I write, and today's headlines featured the partisan snubbing that occurred at last night's State of the Union address.) Some hail Donald Trump as a no-nonsense Washington outsider. To others, he is like the evil Voldemort from the Harry Potter series: "He Who Must Not Be Named."

Whatever our political persuasions, we often invest messianic hope in our political figures. We want them to ensure a more prosperous tomorrow and establish permanent peace. Such were the political overtones of John 12 when the crowd waved palm branches to welcome Jesus into Jerusalem.[1] They were hailing him, but not just as a religious figure or a wonder-worker. They were hailing him as king.

As the crowd chanted in chorus "Blessed is he who comes in the name of the Lord," they were quoting from Psalm 118, a psalm that portrays the king of Israel returning to Jerusalem after a military victory, leading a procession to the temple and climbing the altar with the bound animal sacrifice required by Mosaic law.

As Christians later came to understand, this psalm foreshadowed the work of Jesus, who was not just the king bringing with him the festal sacrifice. He was also the lamb![2]

Singing their hosannas, these onlookers took their (unwitting) place in the long line of witnesses testifying to the truth of Jesus's identity in John's Gospel: John the Baptist, the works of Jesus, the voice of the Father, the testimony of the Scriptures, Jesus's own words, those who'd witnessed the raising of Lazarus. In unison, these voices proclaimed that Jesus was sent from God and that he *was* God. Nevertheless, one massive stumbling block to faith in Jesus remained. It was the cross that he would soon suffer.

Throughout his public ministry, Jesus has been speaking of his hour—and now it's here, the time for fulfilling the purpose for which he has been sent. The Book of Signs is now closing, and the Book of the Passion is now opening. Like the serpent that was lifted up in the wilderness as a means of healing and salvation for the wandering Jews, Jesus will be lifted up on a cross.[3] The cross is the symbol of everything that's upside down about the kingdom that Jesus is bringing. It's a renunciation of worldly power and a refusal of worldly glory. It is a *scandal* in the words of the apostle Paul.[4] But the cross is not just weakness and ignominy. Paradoxically, on the cross, God will exert his greatest authority. He will judge the politics of evil. As Jesus is lifted up, the powers of sin and death will be thrown down. This will be his *glory*.

Some will see the cross—and yet miss its essential meaning. They will have eyes that don't see, hearts that don't understand. Their unbelief and blindness will mirror the unbelief and blindness of the Israelites in the wilderness. Moses had said to them before they entered the promised land, "You have seen all that the LORD did before your eyes in the land of Egypt. . . . But to this day the LORD has not given you a heart to understand or eyes to see or ears to hear."[5] In other words, there is a seeing that isn't believing, a hearing that isn't understanding. Faith is a kind of divinely endowed sixth sense, and it requires trust and surrender—ultimately to Jesus.

In John, we come to understand that our relationship to Jesus is like his relationship to the Father. His obedience is our obedience; his cross is our cross. Like Jesus, we will gain our ultimate freedom through obedience, and it's as we lose our lives that we will find them in the end. I don't want to pretend that this losing of our lives for the sake of Christ is always easy or that this cross is never heavy. Even for Jesus, the cross was cause for inner turmoil and anguish. Still, he shows us that the way of obedience, however seemingly hard, is always the reliable path to life, even eternal gain.[6]

Obedience is the central theme of the book of Deuteronomy; Moses had promised the people of Israel that they would secure the land if they obeyed God's voice. But as Moses came to the end of his life, God revealed that Israel would never be capable of keeping the commands of God. They were bent toward treachery, and despite the many warnings of God's prophets, they would continue to be a willful people. We remember that seemingly fatalistic end. The book left us with what appeared to be an irresolvable dilemma: if God wanted his stubborn son, Israel, to enjoy his blessings, God would have to either relax the demands of the covenant or make it possible, somehow, for his people to meet them.

John's Gospel sheds further light on that dilemma and Deuteronomy's promise of a "circumcised heart." The blessings of *obedience* in Deuteronomy are the blessings of the *Obedient One* in John. Jesus is the perfect law keeper on our behalf. He has perfectly loved his Father with his heart, soul, mind, and strength. He has perfectly loved his neighbor as himself. He has kept the whole commandment of God, and now the blessings of his obedience are available to those who would believe in him. He is the greater Moses, leading his people into the land. He is the Word of God by which every man lives.[7]

To be a Christian is to make a habit of confessing that we are law breakers, not law keepers. To be a Christian is to make a habit of admitting that Jesus, and his cross, are our only hope.

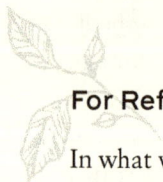

For Reflection/Discussion

In what ways do we miss the real truth about Jesus because of our own misguided expectations? How is the meaning of the cross a hope for you?

DAY 32

Read John 13:1–38 (Focus: vv. 1–5)

Key Verse: "For I have given you an example, that you also should do just as I have done to you." (v. 15)

Undercover Boss

With the exception of my five years as a high school teacher, I've been my own boss for most of my adult working life. I've never been privy to the machinations of office politics, although my husband, a corporate executive, comes home and delivers an earful about the jealousies and strutting ambitions.

As a boss, my husband meets with a lot of obvious flattery. Truthfully, he's glad when people don't take him all that seriously. Once, when the company gym closed, he and some of his colleagues got a wonderfully wry letter of complaint from an employee. It was addressed "Dear Big Cheeses."

Boss isn't the most benign word in our cultural vocabulary. It's easy to assume that power will inevitably corrupt, that it will be leveraged to domineer. We assume that power is the antithesis of love, love the antithesis of power.[1] But to open to John 13—and find Jesus kneeling at the feet of his disciples—is to reconsider everything we thought to be true about power. Here, the master performs a servant's menial task and asks his disciples to imitate his humility.

Jesus's act of foot washing foreshadows the cross. Just as Jesus *lays down* his outer garment, then takes it up again, so he, as the

Good Shepherd, will *lay down* his life for the sheep and take it up again.[2] As willingly as Jesus condescends to wrap a servant's towel around his waist, he also voluntarily surrenders his life. The cross has been *purposed* by God. As Jesus's public ministry now concludes, the chapters ahead allow us to overhear his final closed-door conversations with his twelve disciples, which focus on one sign—the cross—and its meaning.[3]

This story of Jesus has been moving in the direction of the cross. The Word came into the world that he had made, and the world refused him welcome. Jesus is not caught by surprise when he is betrayed, arrested, and finally executed, even if, more than once, we find him "troubled" to know that death awaits and that a friend will deliver him into murderous hands. Jesus understands that the cross is not the end of the story. "He had come from God and was going back to God." The cross reminds Christians that suffering never speaks a final word.

It's divine love, not human violence, that ultimately brings Jesus in confrontation with death. Jesus is assured of his Father's love, and this makes it possible for Jesus to give his life freely and unreservedly. Jesus loves the Father and willingly, gladly glorifies the Father by his sacrifice. Jesus also loves humanity to the very "end" of exchanging his life for theirs.

Wrapped in a towel (and later, hanging on a cross), Jesus invites the world not simply to believe in him *but to be served by him*. As we saw clearly in our study of Deuteronomy, there is something hopelessly bent about the human condition. Though we maintain a degree of public respectability in the world—paying our taxes, being decent neighbors, providing the best for our children—we cannot maintain unswerving loyalty to the God who made us and the God who deserves our worship, no matter how hard we try.

Biblically speaking, sin is not simply language for naming our moral wrongs and faults. It's vocabulary for addressing the infinite gap between our corruption and God's holiness. As sinners, we need a "bath," a cleansing, a baptism, a rebirth. The good news of the gospel is that God's love for the broken world is so fierce, so resolute, so bent on grace and mercy that God himself will endure the humiliation of the cross to purify a people for himself.[4] He will bend to wash our feet, even in his own blood.

Remarkably, Jesus's love as demonstrated in John 13 is not just love for friends. It is also love for enemies. We're told that at this last meal with his disciples, Judas held an esteemed position at the table beside Jesus. His dirty feet might have been the first in Jesus's basin. Jesus passes him the bread of fellowship before Judas disappears into the night, his treasonous plan hatched. But Judas isn't the only betrayer reclining at the table that evening. We learn that Peter, too, will forsake Jesus at a crucial moment, denying to have ever known him.

We must pay attention to the drama as John sketches it. It has three important players: God, humanity, and the devil, or Satan. According to John, Judas is not a rogue figure, acting alone. It's Satan who inspires his evil scheme of betrayal. Although John did not begin his Gospel as his three peers did—with Jesus in the wilderness, facing the temptation of Satan—he has given as much credence to the powers and principalities of evil as Matthew, Mark, and Luke have. Each of the Gospel writers believed in real, personal forces of evil—and in an adversary who stands opposed to God and his kingdom projects. They also believed that the cross was the defeat of those forces of evil—the ultimate "exorcism" of Satan.[5]

I get that mention of the "devil" might become the occasion for skeptical eye-rolling. But anyone who has grappled with the real and recent horrors of human history—the Holocaust, the war in the former Yugoslavia in the 1990s, the Rwandan genocide—is forced to grapple with human depravity. Is it enough to say that the rape and killing of young children is *wrong*? That the systematic extinction of the Jews was *criminal*? That neighbor terrorizing tribal neighbor is merely a violation of the principle of *harm*? Or do we need a word like *evil* to try penetrating the depths of our broken condition?

The love of God is not a sentimentalizing force in the world. It doesn't sing endless rounds of "Kum ba yah" while the world burns. At the cross, the love of God not only embraces the world. It also confronts evil and judges it.

For Reflection/Discussion

What keeps you from having Christ "serve" you? How readily do you acknowledge the reality of invisible, personal powers of evil in the world?

DAY 33

Read John 14:1–31 (Focus: vv. 1–7)

Key Verse: "I am the way, and the truth, and the life. No one comes to the Father except through me." (v. 6)

Last Will and Testament

Many years after the death of my father, I finally gathered some of his papers that my mother had been storing in her garage and brought them home to Toronto, determining to go through them slowly. Because he died when I was only eighteen, this close reading of his work—his poems, his letters, his screenplays, his works of fiction—was intended as an act of meeting my father as much as an act of remembering him. Early into the task, I found a query letter that he wrote to a magazine editor, attached to what must have been one of his first short stories. That typewritten letter brought to life the ambitious twenty-something man that my father must surely have once been.

After someone dies, we treasure their words with greater intensity. This was surely true of Jesus's disciples. Jesus had seen his death coming and spent the final hours before his arrest talking and praying with the eleven young men who had left behind everything to follow him: their livelihoods, families, and homes. These men had followed this itinerant rabbi around Galilee and Judea. They had nurtured high hopes for his career, and his reference to his impending death was no doubt a source of confusion, sadness, even indignation.

"Let not your hearts be troubled," Jesus reassures his friends. At the time, the disciples, like Thomas and Philip, did not clearly perceive the divine purpose in the death of Jesus. The dim-wittedness of their faith, even with all his plain speaking, persisted until the resurrection.[1] But we can't be too hard on the disciples. Though the truth about Jesus is simple enough for a child to understand, it is also a bottomless ocean of complexity. In fact, centuries after Jesus's death, the church would return, time and again, to John 14 (as well as other passages) to understand and articulate the triune nature of God: Father, Son, and Holy Spirit. In a process that took centuries, they rigorously examined the authoritative writings of Christian tradition and eventually landed on language to express the truth that God is both one and three.

We might wonder why God didn't prepare glossaries, diagrams, and step-by-step instructions for his disciples before his death. Why did he leave important truths vulnerable to misunderstanding? But strong-arm tactics have never been God's way. From the very beginning of time, God has endowed his people with real authority and real freedom.[2] Theology is part of the "power" that God has shared with his people, and it invites us into the work of making sense of who he is and what it means to be in relationship with him. Of course, we aren't unaided in this task of sounding the depths of Christian truth. We trust Jesus for the giving of the Holy Spirit, the third person of God who teaches and reminds of all that Jesus said.

The Trinity is a profound (though not explicit) truth illuminated in John 14. But this chapter doesn't only traffic in difficult ideas. It also puts forward plain ones—namely, that Jesus is unique and that his claims are exclusive. Just as Israel was invited to worship one God and him alone, John is inviting us to believe in Yahweh's one Messiah and him alone. To put it into wilderness terms that the Israelites would have understood, Jesus is the way to the promised land, he is the truth given to guide God's people along the way, and most importantly, he's *the land*—in him are all the blessings of life that have been promised to God's people.

To follow the vertical beam of the cross is to remember that there is only one way to know God and to be received by him as his child. We must let Jesus serve us. We must admit that we are sinners and believe that Jesus is the Lamb of God who takes away the sins of the world. But to follow the horizontal beam of the cross is to perceive just how wide God's embrace is of the world. There is no one God would exclude from his offer of saving, forgiving love if they would but receive it in the name of his Son Jesus. The gospel bars none from entry.[3]

In the second half of John 14, emphasis is placed on keeping the commandments of Jesus. Here, we might remember the promissory nature of the Ten Commandments given to Moses and the people of God on Mount Sinai. *You shall not steal* was God's pledge to make his people honest. *You shall not commit adultery* was God's pledge to make his people faithful. Here too in John 14, is another pledge God makes to his people: those who love Jesus *shall keep his commandments.*

Curiously, the five words of faith that emerged in Deuteronomy—see, know, live, love, obey—also emerge in John 14. The disciples *see* the Father by *seeing* Jesus; they *know* the Father by *knowing* Jesus. After Jesus's death, they will *see* him again when he is raised from the dead and *know* that he is in the Father and the Father is in him. As Jesus *lives*, they, too, can *live*. And lastly, those who *love* Jesus will also *obey* Jesus—just as Jesus loves the Father and does exactly as he's commanded.

The message of Jesus is both easy and difficult, simple and profound. We can't offer to God anything but our faith in what he's already done.

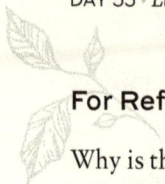

For Reflection/Discussion

Why is the promise of the Holy Spirit such a comfort to Christian believers? What do you personally make of the paradox that the gospel is both radically *exclusive* and radically *inclusive*?

DAY 34

Read John 15:1–27 (Focus: vv. 1–5)

Key Verse: "Whoever abides in me and I in him, he it is that bears much fruit, for apart from me you can do nothing." (v. 5)

The Hard Work of Staying Put

I have never minded the act of planting. I have, however, minded the ongoing, tedious attention that plants demand. Years ago, I wrote a poem for my husband on the occasion of our wedding anniversary. It began with an ode to my horticultural failures:

> I bring home tomato plants in May,
> fall prey to the naiveté
> of yellow bloom.
> I promise to water,
> but it's inattention I will pay,
> breaking promises
> and forcing drought.
> They'll die before July
> with the creep of neglect,
> begging one delicious drink.[1]

In John 15, Jesus announces himself to be the "true vine" and his father the "vinedresser." I'm guessing that most readers, even the green-thumbed ones, are far removed from this image, but it would have been instantly meaningful for any Jewish reader of John's Gospel.

One of the most frequent images for Israel in the Old Testament was as the vine that God had taken from Egypt, replanted in the promised land, and tended with great care.[2] The longstanding disappointment of that vine—that people—was that it never produced the fruit it was intended to. Israel was never the blessing to the world God had called it to be. But as the true vine, Jesus declares himself to be the true Israel, the faithful Son of God. When he gives his life, it will feed the world.

The first lesson to draw from the metaphor of the vine and the branches is about our relationship with God. If sin has to do with habits of autonomy, faith has to do with habits of dependence. As branches, we survive only insofar as we are nourished by the elements of life passing through the vine. To be a Christian implies vital connection to Christ. On the one hand, this is another picture of the intimacy that God has longed to enjoy with his people. In the story of Israel, he made his home in their very midst.[3] He was never cold and aloof, unwilling to be bothered by the tedious affairs of human beings. He drew near.

On the other hand, Deuteronomy also illuminated how few were ultimately afforded real proximity to God. When Moses climbed Mount Sinai and disappeared in the cloud of God's presence, the rest of the nation stood removed. Moses alone talked with God as a friend, face to face.[4] When it came time to offer sacrifices at the temple, the "house of God," only members of the priestly caste were permitted entry. The vast majority of God's people knew God only from a distance.

Through Jesus, we are drawn closer than any of our spiritual ancestors could have imagined. God isn't simply *with* us in the person of Jesus; he lives *in* us through the Holy Spirit. As many of the New Testament writers later picked up, this idea made the physical body of every disciple a temple, the very dwelling place of God.[5] At God's initiative, he has made his home in us and invites us to make our home in and with him.

This life of abiding in the vine is characterized not by exhausting religious practice but by rest. It is an "easy yoke" and a "light burden."[6] At the same time, resting in Jesus and relying on his work is hardly an automatic response, and *abide* might be the most countercultural command. Isn't it true that the majority of us recognize ourselves more in motion than at rest? It takes intention to stay connected to the vine. If we don't deliberately structure our days to create the conditions for abiding in Jesus and letting his words abide in us, it simply won't happen. Hurry and distraction will be our default settings.

This book has been an invitation to abide: to lay aside some of our daily franticness and let the words of Jesus abide in us. It's not been meant as the "effort" of cataloging more ideas about God. This immersion into the Bible has invited us to find and follow Jesus, to make his friendship the still point in our tilting, turning world.

The second lesson of the vine is this: if the life of the Christian is inwardly nourished by its connection to Jesus, it is also outwardly productive. It bears fruit. It *feeds.* Of course, we feed only insofar as we have been fed. What Jesus does here is abolish any neat distinction between the contemplative life and the activist one, between spiritual experience and social responsibility. To be connected to Jesus, living in constant conversation with the indwelling Word of God, ensures that we become people actively committed to the good of our neighbor.

The word *world* is one that John is uniquely fond of. He uses it to talk about the realm that rejects God's reign, that prefers darkness to light. As disciples of Jesus, we're not "of the world." Instead, we are apprenticed into the way that is Jesus, the truth that is Jesus, the life that is Jesus. His methods are our methods, his priorities our priorities. But neither are we *against* the world, even when it remains hostile to us. To be a disciple of Jesus is to be zealously *for* the good of the world. Just as Jesus was sent to give his life for the world, Jesus has sent his people on a similar mission of both love and witness.

In fact, it's love that *is* our witness. We know from church historians that in the first centuries after Jesus's death, his disciples had no airtight business plan for storming the globe with the gospel. Rather, their love drew people to desire to be a part of their community. "According to [early church father] Tertullian, the outsiders looked at the Christians and saw them energetically feeding poor people and burying them, caring for boys and girls who lacked property and parents, and being attentive to aged slaves and prisoners."[7] Jesus's followers loved as Jesus loved, and it piqued the world's curiosity.

Abide in Jesus: in his love, in his words, in him. It's a profoundly simple, often practically hard, habit of faith.

For Reflection/Discussion

What keeps us so inordinately busy that "abiding in Jesus" feels like really hard advice? How have you experienced the connection between abiding in Jesus and feeding the world with your life?

DAY 35

Read John 16:1–33 (Focus: vv. 4–11)

Key Verse: "I have said these things to you, that in me you may have peace. In the world you will have tribulation. But take heart; I have overcome the world." (v. 33)

The Helper

At a Christian camp the summer before my junior year of high school, I decided to follow Jesus. I remember the first time, after that week, that I saw many of my school friends who were not yet informed of this abrupt change—this "rebirth." A large group of us met at a crowded movie theater, and after the movie I drove home, fighting an overwhelming feeling of loneliness.

In my bedroom that night, I played a familiar version of Bible roulette. I didn't go looking for any particular verse, only let my Bible fall open to John 16 and my finger drift across the page. It fell on verse 33, and once I'd read it, the darkness subsided. Jesus promised that while I'd have trouble in this world, I'd also have peace.

This reassurance of peace in the midst of trouble is among the last words that Jesus spoke to his disciples, and they sound strikingly similar to the parting blessing that Moses pronounced over the people of Israel before his own death. For both communities, the deaths of their leaders would arrive like death blows. Moses, of course, had the advantage of commissioning Joshua to lead as his successor. By contrast, Jesus is left to anticipate that at the moment of his arrest, the disciples will cowardly scatter.[1]

As the disciples grapple with the truth that Jesus is leaving them, if only for a "little while," Jesus promises his physical absence will be for their ultimate good. Several times, he speaks of joy, which surely seems misplaced when a funeral is at hand. But as Jesus insists, only in his absence can he send the Helper, the third person of the Trinity. Jesus does not intend to leave his disciples alone in the world.

As the late Lesslie Newbigin noticed, if it weren't for the sending of God's Spirit, the Christian church might have easily turned into a mausoleum. If Jesus had belonged only to the past, we might find ourselves cherishing "his chair, his slippers, his spectacles."[2] We'd venerate him as the leader of a movement—and as a memory. Instead, Jesus promised that he would return and be present through his Spirit. Through the Holy Spirit, the speaking ministry of God would continue as he illuminated the "many things" which Jesus longed to say to his disciples at the end of his life, things for which there wasn't sufficient time and understanding.

In the book of Acts, which records the birth of the Christian church after Jesus was raised from the dead, we see many aspects of the fulfillment of Jesus's promise. In Acts 2 on the day of Pentecost, the disciples were filled with the Holy Spirit and miraculously endowed with the gift of speaking in foreign languages. Everyone at this feast heard, each in their own language, the message of the gospel: Jesus had been crucified, buried, and raised from the dead.

Another visible fulfillment of Jesus's promise was realized through the writings of the apostles, which were received by the early church as Scripture.[3] The Holy Spirit breathed the words of Jesus into the pages of their biographies and letters, even this Gospel that we've been reading, and he continues to speak through this "living and active" book.[4]

The present-tense speaking ministry of the Holy Spirit explains why we can search the Bible for wisdom to help decide our contemporary questions. The Holy Spirit makes it possible for God to speak to his people through the Bible in the same way that God spoke to Israel through Moses, actively leading them. God's people today are much like those wilderness wanderers, and as they "travel this road, they will meet wholly new situations, new peoples, new cultures, new structures which the 'ruler of the world' has devised to embody his claim to power. . . . The Spirit of truth will show them the way to go."[5]

The only question to ask is, Are we listening?

Just as the Holy Spirit will guide the people of God into the truth of God, he will also convict the world of their guilt. They stand convicted for their sin, which has everything to do with their posture toward Jesus. They haven't believed in him. They've declared him guilty. They've perceived the cross as his defeat rather than his victory. The Holy Spirit assumes a prosecutorial role, which underscores that God isn't impressed by the sincerity of our religious opinions. He values our commitment to the truth as revealed in Jesus, and it remains his prerogative to judge according to that truth.

The Gospel of John affirms that the *truth* of the Christian faith is to be found in the historical reality of Jesus's life, death, and resurrection: this *seeing* of the Lord.[6] In one of his letters, the apostle John adds his own eyewitness experience of these events to the proclamation of the gospel: "That which was from the beginning, which we have heard, which we have seen with our eyes, which we looked upon and have touched with our hands, concerning the word of life—the life was made manifest, and we have seen it."[7] The apostles didn't preach a self-help message. They boldly preached the bodily resurrection of Jesus Christ, and as the book of Acts records, the disciples were met with raging hostility, even death, just as Jesus foretold. In the end, ten were martyred, and John was exiled on the island of Patmos.[8]

As followers of Jesus, we will surely face persecution as the disciples did. But the good news is this: we're never alone. Jesus is cheering us on, and his Spirit is our source of ongoing strength and help.

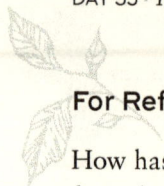

For Reflection/Discussion

How has the Holy Spirit been at work in you throughout these forty days to guide you into truth? What fears do you have about facing persecution or rejection for your faith in Jesus?

DEBORAH SMITH

"He called me to love what I used to hate and hate what I used to love."

As a child, Deborah Smith attended services at the Southern church that her great-grandfather built, the church that her many aunts and uncles and cousins attended as well. Her mother was a Christian believer though her dad, one of the first black news anchors in North Carolina, was not. At the age of ten, Deborah's idyllic childhood unraveled one Sunday when, after church and lunch at her grandmother's house, she, her mom, and her three brothers came home to find their father gone.

After the family migrated to the DC suburbs in Maryland, they stopped attending church regularly, although Deborah's mother instilled Christian values and taught the Bible to her children. Deborah was a good student, a smart kid. But she began using drugs in middle school and became sexually promiscuous in high school. "I know I heard the gospel growing up, over and over again," Deborah admits. Still, her religious head knowledge didn't prevent her further descent into hard-core drugs and the choice to have two abortions. "It was a vicious cycle: drugs, men, despair, go to church," she tells me during our video call. "I would want to get my life together. Then I'd have these periods of abstinence where I wasn't doing drugs, where I was living a productive life. But it never lasted. It was always short-lived." Between the ages of twenty and thirty-three, Deborah managed to hold down respectable jobs at corporate law firms, often returning to church to walk the aisle, crying but resisting real change. "I just wanted the pain of my sins removed."

After being terminated from a law firm in downtown DC, Deborah was sent by a temporary employment agency to work at a prestigious firm in Georgetown. "I was cleaned up and feeling good." But despite her sobriety, Deborah felt the overwhelming and sudden desire to contact her drug dealer. He fronted her some drugs on credit, and for three days, in the grip of her addiction, Deborah failed to show up at the temporary job she'd hoped would become permanent. Knowing that she would need her paycheck to pay for the drugs, she went back to the office with a tragic story to excuse her absence. "[My manager] was in tears as I told her I had been kidnapped for three days by my ex-boyfriend who held me hostage in the house. She gave me all this crisis information and told me to take a few days off. I never went back. That was a Wednesday." The next day, Deborah sold her car for drugs. By Saturday, the bottom fell out entirely.

It was January 16, 1999. An ice storm had shut down DC, making it impossible for Deborah to leave the house. "That's a nightmare for a drug addict." She hadn't eaten for days, and she realized, with new clarity, that she might very well die, alone and cold, dressed only in her undergarments. "It was just a disgusting sense of desperation that I felt."

Deborah continues, "It was at that moment when I cried out to the Lord in a state of humility I'd never felt before. I knew I was going to die. I knew I was in a situation, in a hopeless dilemma that I could not fix. I had wanted to stop and change my life years before I was able to stop and change my life." She prayed to the

God she'd learned about all those years growing up in church, her legs dangling from the pew. "Help me, God. I don't want to die this way. I know you're real; I know you love me." After what felt like only minutes, her brother knocked on the door, and she answered, shivering. "Get your things. We're getting out of here," her brother said.

Deborah's brother drove her to her father's house and looked for a bed for her at a local treatment center. "I just slept and ate. I was like a baby bird that had been found in the snow with a broken wing." Deborah remembered the curious looks of her younger half-sister and half-brother as they peeked through the bedroom door when someone opened it to bring her food. "I remember thinking, *You're coming back to life.*" Deborah waited two weeks for a bed at a treatment center and, what she describes as only a miraculous intervention from God, stayed clean the entire time. "Who goes into a treatment center clean? It makes no sense. But I did not want to use drugs."

Forty-five days later, Deborah was fully detoxed and moved into a sober-living center. There, she met a Christian minister who took her through the Gospel of Matthew and the Gospel of John. Only then did she realize what had really happened to her. "All of the gospel that I had heard growing up, all the church, all the Scriptures"—they had prepared Deborah to cry out to the Lord and have faith enough to believe that he might hear. "It was like this light bulb went on, and I understood what it meant to have been so far off. When I cried out, it was him running to me, like the father ran to the prodigal in almost a disgraceful way. He ran to me and did something that was very obviously him because I could never have stopped using drugs on my own. I could not muster up enough shame for the way that I was living." She knew that God's power was at work in her life because once she had lived for drugs—and now she was living without any desire for them.

"He saved me. He rescued me. He put his Spirit in me. He called me to love what I used to hate and hate what I used to love. There's no doubt in my mind that he's real. Despite all those years of wretchedness, I walk confidently in the proof that I am a new creation!"

She wants her story to be evidence that God's arm is long and that there is no one beyond his saving reach. She is fifty-four, single, and "very content in that singleness. I do desire a husband," she tells me. "But more than that, I really want what the Lord has for me."

Deborah Smith joyfully serves at Anacostia River Church in DC where she leads women's Bible studies. She works as the events manager and outreach coordinator for Christian Legal Aid in the District of Columbia.

DAY 36

Read John 17:1–26 (*Focus: vv. 11–19*)

Key Verse: "As you sent me into the world, so I have sent them into the world." (*v.* 18)

The Lord's Prayer

When my children were still quite young, I led a neighborhood Bible study on the Lord's Prayer. For almost a year, we met every other week to explore Jesus's familiar prayer, phrase by phrase, and apply its meaning to our lives. "Our Father, who art in heaven, hallowed be your name . . ." We talked about worry, about money, about forgiveness, about sin, about trusting God for all things.

When we think of the Lord's Prayer, we rightly think of the prayer that begins "Our Father," recorded in its fullest version by Matthew.[1] John, however, does not choose to include any version of this "Lord's Prayer" in his Gospel. Still, in one important sense, John 17 is a kind of "Lord's Prayer." Jesus isn't teaching the disciples how to pray. He is himself praying, and we overhear this intimate conversation with his Father.

This is the last of three moments in John's Gospel where we find Jesus praying. In chapter 11, Jesus stands beside the tomb of Lazarus and lifts his eyes to heaven to audibly pray. He thanks God for hearing his prayer, admitting that he voices his prayer aloud more for the benefit of those standing around than for himself. Jesus calls Lazarus from the tomb, and in that moment, it becomes instantly clear that the prayers of Jesus are effective.

This becomes the basis of the confidence that Jesus commends to the disciples (and to us) when we pray. If Jesus's prayers are heard and answered, surely the prayers we offer in Jesus's name are also heard and answered. This doesn't mean that we get everything we want from God just because we've prayed for it.[2] Instead, as we pray, we look to have our will conformed to God's will. To pray in the name of Jesus is to ask according to Jesus's priorities and to trust God's gladness in answering.

A second occasion of Jesus praying is in chapter 12, right after his triumphal entry into Jerusalem. There, Jesus counts the cost of the obedience he must offer to his father, which is his own life.[3] "And what shall I say? 'Father, save me from this hour'? But for this purpose I have come to this hour. Father, glorify your name."[4] As Jesus's prayer demonstrates, prayer isn't just the audacious act of asking God for impossible things. It's also the act of surrendering to what seems to be God's impossible asking.

Prayer is a two-way conversation. We don't just lob our wish list to heaven like it is an Amazon fulfillment center. We remain committed to hearing whatever God will say, whatever God will ask, wherever God will lead. As Ben Jolliffe, pastor of Resurrection Church in Ottawa, once preached, the tension of prayer—and faith—lies at the heart of the opening phrase of the Lord's Prayer: "Our Father who art in heaven, hallowed be your name." *Our Father* is the confidence we have in prayer: God is good and does good on behalf of his children. We can want what God wants because we know God wants our good. But as an important counterweight, *hallowed be your name* is the reverence we have in prayer: God is holy, other, set apart, and obligated to no one but himself. To know that God is holy chastens what we might ask of him.

In this third and final prayer, Jesus prays for his disciples, including the eleven who remain but also those who will follow him in every generation to come. He prays for their (and our) unity and for their (and our) protection from the evil one. Jesus is praying for his church. He wants it to flourish because it will be the church's job, by the power of the Holy Spirit, to bear living witness to his reality. The church is sent as Jesus has been sent. The church is sanctified as Jesus is sanctified. The church is the agent of God's ongoing mission of saving love.

When Jesus prayed for Lazarus to be raised, it was easy to see that God answered him. By contrast, it's not all that apparent that God was listening as closely when Jesus prayed for the church. We can't help but think of the failures of the church throughout the centuries: violence, abuse, corruption, hypocrisy, hatred, self-righteousness, indifference. The sins of the church are many—yet in his prayer, Jesus seems remarkably hopeful for his church, even that he might be "glorified" in his people. Was he wrong?

Athanasius was an early church father who wrote about the "glory" of God's people, made possible through the work of Jesus and the presence of his Spirit in them. He wrote of Christians' radical commitment to peace and patience in a barbaric age as well as their pledge to sexual chastity in an epoch of sexual license. He believed that Christians bore the light of their Savior, Jesus.

The church has many vices—but it also has virtues. In fact, Christianity has been largely responsible for many of our current social values. "The early Christian insistence on brotherhood across racial and ethnic boundaries, even across the dichotomy of slave and free, became a spark to ignite a new moral imagination. . . . Values that many of us in the West today consider to be universal and independent of religious thought turn out not to have sprung from the ground during the Enlightenment but to have grown from the gradual spread and influence of Christian beliefs."[5] We don't value equality and justice and protection for the most vulnerable because these are intuitive virtues. These ethics are distinctly Christian.

Jesus prays—and we discover what he loved and wished to protect. Jesus prays—and we also discover the world as Jesus saw it, warring with the powers and principalities of darkness. Most importantly, prayer prepares Jesus to face his darkest hour.

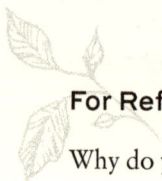

For Reflection/Discussion

Why do you think Jesus is as hopeful for the church as he is? How have you seen evidence of the beauty of Jesus's church?

DAY 37

Read John 18:1–40 (Focus: vv. 33–38)

Key Verse: "My kingdom is not of this world. If my kingdom were of this world, my servants would have been fighting, that I might not be delivered over to the Jews." (v. 36)

The Gospel Garden

Anne Lamott is the author of *Bird by Bird*, and many writers have come to rely on her straight-shooting advice. "Tell your stories," she insists. "If people wanted you to write warmly about them, they should have behaved better." This isn't a rule I've usually followed, and when I have, I've mostly come to regret it. Our narration of the past, however objective we try to be, is inevitably a reconstruction. The facts never speak entirely for themselves. We cull them, we arrange them, and this makes the task of memory an interpretive one.

As divinely inspired Scripture, John's Gospel is not subjected to the frailties of human memory or bias, and the Evangelist took no liberties to embellish the facts of Jesus's story. Nevertheless, John has shaped his historical record for a very particular theological purpose, which he reveals at the end of his Gospel. He wants his readers to conclude that "Jesus is the Christ, the Son of God, and that by believing [they] may have life in his name."[1] With his thesis in mind, he selects and omits material, artfully arranging his content for the purpose of persuading his readers on this point: the "life" Moses proclaimed to Israel was now on offer in and through Jesus Christ.

It's important that we clearly understand the meaning of the title "Son of God" to grasp this Gospel's main point. It is not simply a reference to Jesus's divine nature but also to his royal identity. In ancient Judaism, "Son of God" was a decidedly political title, one reserved for the king of Israel.[2] In ancient Roman culture, "Son of God" was also a title given to the emperor. In the next two chapters of John, Jesus's kingly rule will become much more prominent, especially as we hear Pilate pose, multiple times, this pressing question: "Are you the King of the Jews?"

As New Testament scholar N. T. Wright sees it, all four Gospels tell the story of how God became king.[3] The surprise, of course, is that Jesus is not coronated with pomp and circumstance but at the site of his own crucifixion. When Jesus became king, hanging on a cross, he brought to completion a story that began in a primordial garden—when God ruled as king over his creation and his subjects, Adam and Eve. In that kingdom, God's rule was benevolent, and he invited humanity to receive his many good gifts, including the fruit of every tree in the garden but one.

Importantly, that first garden was not a democracy; it was a kingdom. Blessings were enjoyed, but obedience was also expected. When Adam and Eve refused to pledge their loyalties to the King, they were banished from the kingdom and sent to wander beyond its walls. This is humanity's great tragedy as the Bible tells it: our preference for autonomy has ensured not our freedom but our curse. Knowledge of this ancient story can inform our reading today. If the first Adam failed in a garden, the second Adam will not. He will surrender himself to God—and to the arresting soldiers—for God's purposes.

According to the Bible, God the King does not exercise autocratic power but instead rules by love. In chapter 10 of his Gospel, John recorded Jesus's teaching on the good shepherd, that he would be the one to lay down his life for his sheep, that he would not run away, as the hired hand would, at the sight of the robber. Now, as Jesus is delivered into the hands of the Jewish leaders—and by their hands into the hands of Pilate, the Roman governor—it's clear that these leaders are the failed shepherds condemned in much of the Old Testament and alluded to by Jesus in that earlier chapter of John. "This is a story of religious corruption," writes New Testament scholar Gary Burge.[4] Annas and Caiaphas maneuver to protect their power, even at the cost of an innocent man's life. They cherish political expediency in the name of God. But as Jesus reminds Pilate (and as John reminds us), the kingdom that he brings does not operate according to the normal rules of power brokering. In fact, as he allows himself to be crucified, willingly drinking the cup of wrath that his Father has given to him, he will prove the mystery of the gospel: God's power is made perfect in weakness.[5] The cross is not the defeat of the kingdom but the great vindication and victory of Jesus the King.

Jesus won't settle for being anything less than King over his followers, and faith in Jesus demands every square inch of our lives. He wants the ultimate authority to guide our lives in decisions both big and small: where we live, whom we marry, what career we pursue, how we spend our money and time. It's not that Jesus is a micromanager, unnecessarily sticking his nose into the details. It's just that life is lived in the details—not just in the notable moments performed in public and recorded for posterity but in the moments at the breakfast table, in the car, and on the sidelines of the soccer field. Just as Moses told Israel that belonging to God demanded complete and careful obedience to God, Jesus insists the same thing when he takes the title of King. There is no "faith" in Jesus that is mere Sunday morning lip service.

Jesus is a king we can serve willingly. In his kingdom, obedience is freedom, not constraint; it is blessing, not curse. King Jesus does not exercise power for his own pleasure. He is eager to protect his disciples, not willing that they should suffer harm when his accusers storm the garden to arrest him. He is a king with authority, but his authority is resolutely expressed in self-sacrificing, serving love.

Faith is the habit of trusting that whatever King Jesus commands and wherever King Jesus leads, it will be good.

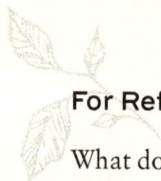

For Reflection/Discussion

What do you think it means when Jesus says to Pilate, "My kingdom is not of this world"? Where do you sense your own resistance to the idea of Jesus's kingly authority over your life?

DAY 38

Read John 19:1–42 (Focus: vv. 28–37)

Key Verse: "For these things took place that the Scripture might be fulfilled." (*v. 36*)

The Finish Line

A small card that a friend gave me a couple of years ago fell out of a reference book today. On the card, there is a small ink drawing of a red-headed woodpecker. Beside the bird is written: "Even the woodpecker owes his success to the fact that he uses his head and keeps on pecking away until he finishes the job."

I'll confess that I'm given to fits and starts in work and life. I find it easier to begin than to finish, to launch than to complete. It's why I'm convinced that most acts of heroism can be found after mile 26, when we feel ourselves limping across the finish line.

"It is finished." At the climactic point of his narrative, John records these important words from the dying Jesus at the very moment he draws his last agonized breath. His words are a period, not a comma. They are a pronouncement of completion. Jesus has accomplished the work that God sent him to do.

As we arrive at the crucifixion, we would be wrong to see the bruised and bloodied Jesus as a victim. At every turn, he has freely followed the road to Golgotha.[1] In fact, as the record of events bears out, Scripture has predicted many of the details of Jesus's death: his betrayal, the soldiers' bartering for his clothes, his unbroken bones, his pierced side, his thirst slaked by sour wine. The cross was no interruption to God's plan. It *was* the plan.

For the first time, Gospel writer John makes mention of his own eyewitness testimony that he has contributed to this account. This beloved disciple, along with four women, stands near enough to the cross to receive some of Jesus's final instructions for the care of his mother, Mary. Though something cosmic is happening on the cross—as Jesus accomplishes the salvation of humanity—something very intimate and familial is happening too. Jesus the Savior is also Jesus the son.

The crucifixion of Jesus is the climax of John's Gospel and the lynchpin of Christian faith. Of course, there have long been theories that Jesus merely swooned at the cross or that his death and subsequent resurrection are meant to be understood metaphorically rather than literally. But that's a sloppy reading of every Gospel account, including John's, which carefully establishes the reality of Jesus's physical death, verified by Roman soldiers. They do not break his legs, as they normally would to hasten the death of the crucified, but instead they pierce his side. The death leaves behind a body, which is taken down from the cross on the eve of the Sabbath and prepared for burial by two Jewish leaders, Joseph and Nicodemus. These men would have had every opportunity, presumably every incentive, to deny the death of Jesus, especially when in three days' time, his disciples begin preaching his resurrection.

Given that crucifixion was a form of public humiliation and degradation, the disciples themselves would have had reason for papering over this scandalous history. What leader worth following is hung on a Roman cross, a form of execution normally reserved for slaves, foreigners, and criminals? "Think how loyalty would burn to right this wrong, to clear his memory, to save his reputation, to prove that gross outrage had been done him, to magnify the life so that the death might be forgotten. . . . But nothing of the kind seems to have occurred to the Evangelists. They literally glory in the Cross."[2] The preaching of the apostles reflects their commitment to the cross and its meaning.

Christians across the centuries have mined the Gospel accounts of the cross for many different Old Testament images and metaphors, but in John's Gospel, he seems especially interested in focusing on Jesus as the Passover Lamb. The feast of Passover, and the slaughtered lamb at its center, is rooted in the story of Israel's deliverance from Egyptian slavery.[3] Unsuccessfully, Moses had pleaded with Pharaoh on nine different occasions to let the people of Israel go. Each time he had been soundly refused. As a means of judgment, God brought a series of plagues on Egypt to force Pharaoh's hand, but Egypt's leader only grew more stubborn. The tenth of those plagues proved to be the most catastrophic. God promised that every firstborn male son and slave and animal in every Egyptian household would die. The Israelites, however, would be protected by virtue of slaughtering a lamb and painting its blood on the doorposts of their houses. "The blood shall be a sign for you, on the houses where you are. And when I see the blood, I will pass over you, and no plague will befall you to destroy you."[4] It's the blood of the lamb that saved Israel—and it's the blood of Jesus that saves us. Jesus is the perfect, unblemished sacrifice: "The Lamb of God, who takes away the sins of the world."[5]

As we've already noted, the slaughtered Passover Lamb is, however shockingly, also a king. The title that hangs over this cross—Jesus of Nazareth, the King of the Jews—is an imperial proclamation. It announces to the Jews (in Aramaic), to the Romans (in Latin), and to the rest of the Mediterranean world (in Greek) that Jesus is King. Just as we learned in Deuteronomy that the God of Israel was the God of gods and the Lord of lords, sovereign over every nation, so Jesus is King over all of humanity. When he is buried by Joseph and Nicodemus, his burial is fit for a king.[6]

This one who promised to be living water, slaking the thirst of every human being, is now poured out on the cross. He thirsts. It could seem like the tragic end of one man's life and the movement he tried to launch. But the story doesn't end there.

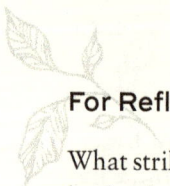

For Reflection/Discussion

What strikes you as important in John's account of the crucifixion, both what he chose to include and what he might have left out? If Jesus is indeed the Passover Lamb, taking away the sins of the world, what does that mean for our guilt and shame?

DAY 39

Read John 20:1–31 (Focus: vv. 1–10)

Key Verse: "Now Jesus did many other signs in the presence of his disciples, which are not written in this book." (*v. 30*)

Closing Arguments

At the time of writing this, my son, Nathan, is a graduating high school senior. Ryan and I might have once worried about his diffident attitudes toward school, but all that changed last year when Mr. Binder became his English teacher. Suddenly, Nathan was voraciously reading not only the assigned texts from class but the optional ones as well. As Nathan's intellectual curiosities have grown, so too have his spiritual questions. He's coming to understand that the habits of faith must be his, not ours.

Everyone must decide for themselves who Jesus is and whether to follow him. Throughout his Gospel, John has begged his readers to consider historical facts. In John 20, he is lining up another "exhibit" in Jesus's extended trial. In addition to the seven signs, or miracles, that he's recorded in his Gospel, he now offers evidence for the bodily resurrection of Jesus—the eighth, and greatest, sign. Just as Jesus was verified to be physically dead in John 19, Jesus was equally verified to have risen from the dead by numerous eyewitnesses in John 20.

John's account does not read like propaganda. Conspicuously absent from John's record is the razzle-dazzle of legend that showed up in later apocryphal gospels—where Jesus is resurrected in luminous power and blinding glory. Instead, John's version has an understated quality to it. In fact, as it tells the story, the empty tomb does not immediately compel Jesus's disciples to belief. Rather, they are slow to understand the significance of his missing body.

There are a variety of elements in John's narrative that confirm the historicity of his account. First, there are the seemingly incidental details of the linen burial cloths and the face cloth, which assure that no grave robbery has taken place. Second, there are the minor differences in John's account and those of the other Gospel writers. (How many women came to the tomb? How many angels?) If the disciples had wanted to provide incontrovertible evidence for their resurrection accounts, they might have thought to straighten their stories. Most importantly, each of them should have provided more credible witnesses to the resurrection than women, whose testimony would not have been legally admissible at the time.

The story of Jesus's resurrection, as John recounts it, seems to be less what the disciples *wished* to happen and more what really did happen. Moreover, the historical core of the Gospel's resurrection accounts was confirmed by much earlier sources: the creed cited by Paul in 1 Corinthians 15:3–5 and the empty tomb account in Mark. Both of these sources can be dated as early as AD 37 (or earlier), just years after the death of Jesus in AD 30.[1] That's scarcely enough time for the development of more legendary accounts, which inevitably appear later.

It becomes apparent that the resurrection, as with all the other "signs" in John's Gospel, is not a religious claim or a philosophical claim, its "truth" subjectively held in the eye of the beholder. Instead, the resurrection of Jesus is a historical claim, one to be either confirmed or disputed, verified or denied by *living witnesses*. This is Christianity's fundamental uniqueness when compared with other world religions. Its claims are public; its truth is bound up with recorded history.

But even if we could be convinced that Jesus was raised from the dead, what does the resurrection of Jesus mean? Why does it matter that Christians believe that Jesus was not only crucified but also, three days later, risen from the dead? It matters because it attests to the truth of Jesus's identity, the truth that Thomas expresses when he puts his hands into Jesus's scars and wounds and is finally convinced that Jesus is alive: "My Lord and my God!" As God himself, Jesus holds the keys of life and of death. He is not just the one raised from the dead; he is also "the resurrection and the life." The grave has no power over him and his followers, and though their bodies will physically die one day, they can have reliable hope in their own resurrection.[2]

The resurrection also matters because it vindicates not only Jesus's words but also his work, specifically his work on the cross. If we can believe who Jesus is, we can believe what he came to do: take away the sins of the world and give *life* to all who would believe in him. We can begin to understand the reason for Moses's optimism at the end of Deuteronomy: "Happy are you, O Israel!" His blessing is forward-looking as he looks ahead to the work of Christ.[3] The resurrection of Jesus is the proclamation that we have a Savior, one who suffered on behalf of our bent and broken condition and raised us to new life. He gives his Spirit to us that we might indeed become the people of God who *shall* love and obey him.

A closer look at John's verb, "believe," in verse 31 provides us with an enigmatic understanding of the author's purpose. In some manuscripts of John, the tense of this verb is best translated "come to believe." In other manuscripts, however, the verb is best read as "continue believing." That subtle grammatical difference between the various manuscripts begs an important question: Was John writing his Gospel to people not yet committed to Jesus or to people who already called themselves Christians?

Maybe John intended that both the convinced and the curious would read his Gospel. In my own experience at least, faith in

Jesus seems to be something we both "come to" and "continue in." Thomas might be the best example of this kind of faith. He has walked with Jesus for three years and, in chapter 11, even expressed his willingness to die with Jesus. Still, he's not a man who will be easily convinced that Jesus is alive again. He won't believe on the testimony of the disciples alone. No, he must put his hands into the scars and wounds of Jesus. Thomas came to believe—and also needed proofs to continue believing.

John's Gospel, as a record of these eight important "signs" in Jesus's ministry, makes no real apology that we should ask for proofs in our lives of tenuous faith, even if more than proofs will be required.

For Reflection/Discussion

If the evidence for the resurrection of Christ is credible, what real difference will it make in your life? What habits do you need to cultivate in order to "continue in" faith?

DAY 40

Read John 21:1–25 (Focus: vv. 15–19)

Key Verse: "Now there are also many other things that Jesus did. Were every one of them to be written, I suppose that the world itself could not contain the books that would be written." (*v.* 25)

Revelation

Over the course of these last forty days, most of us have probably proven fitful in our commitment to reading the Bible. There have likely been times when we have been preoccupied by life's more apparent urgencies: a sick child, a car repair, a pressing work deadline. Maybe forty days have become forty-five or sixty—or more. Maybe this book has collected dust on the bedside table. Maybe guilt calls us back to it.

Or maybe it's the longing for real faith that acts like a lure. Maybe it's impossible to pretend that we're not hungry for a word from God.

Even if we've kept to our forty-day commitment, we can easily despair when our engagement with the Bible produces little visible result—when it doesn't make us instantaneously more loving, less anxious, more joyful, less fearful. Are we doing it wrong if it doesn't microwave us into saints? But as I've grown to learn, the payoff of reading Scripture is not usually found in the occasional epiphanies, when God thunders with an unmistakable word. The blessing is in the *habit*. Habits reap rewards—but the kind of rewards that require patience to notice, then measure.

In so many areas of our lives, it's the repetitive motions—the habits—that turn out to be most significant. In the life of faith, another important habit, beyond the regular reading of Scripture, is gathering weekly with other Christ-followers. (Sadly, this habit has had to be reimagined in 2020 because of the pandemic.) In my church, we follow the same liturgy for our Sunday service every week: God calls, God cleanses, God communes, God commissions. As we move from the songs of praise to the prayers of confession, from the preaching of Scripture to the prayer of benediction, we move through the story of the gospel.

I see a similar movement in the final chapter of John, where Peter is first called then commissioned. Similar to the ending of Deuteronomy, John's Gospel ends with another *inclusio* in verses 1 and 14. What's being emphasized here is the *revelation* of Jesus to his disciples. His disciples never knew where to look for him after he left Joseph's tomb on Easter morning. Each time he revealed himself, it was an act of grace—especially to Peter, who must face this Jesus whom he betrayed three times.

No doubt Peter expected to hear words of reproach from Jesus. But Jesus did not rehearse his blemished history or scold any other of the disciples. Instead, God called his disciples, including Peter, to his breakfast table. He fed them. Surely as they sat down to their bread and fish, they thought of an earlier meal and another miracle, when Jesus had fed a hungry crowd of thousands and pronounced that any who wished to follow him would have to eat his flesh and drink his blood.

This side of the cross, Jesus's words began to make a lot more sense.

All this talk of revelation means simply this: God wants to be known. This is the "grace upon grace" that John referred to in his opening prologue. It's why God spoke in the garden to create, to bless, and to command. It's why God searched for Adam and for Eve after they'd disobeyed his command: "Where are you?"

It's why God continued speaking, calling Abraham to follow and Moses to lead. Even the law, which God gave to Israel, was a means of grace so that his people might know him and be sure of his will. His commands were always intended as blessings and as an invitation to *life*. And finally, as the Gospel of John has attested, God has willed himself to be most fully known in the person of his Son, Jesus Christ. God clothed himself with flesh and moved into the neighborhood. God's willingness to be known was ultimately the willing of his own death.

There are no lengths to which God will not go to make himself known.

We can't know God apart from his self-revelation, and this is to admit our utter dependence upon his grace. As the fourteenth-century Catholic philosopher and theologian Thomas Aquinas argued, faith that is formed by God's revelation is far more democratic, far more solid than if we were left to our own faculties of logic.[1] Or as Saint Jerome said many centuries earlier, revelation invites us to apprehend the beauty of God's truth, that it is "a pool that is deep enough for scholars to swim in without ever touching bottom and yet shallow enough for children to wade in without ever drowning."[2] God can reveal himself to a child—and God can reveal himself to a PhD. God can reveal himself to an assembly-line worker—and God can reveal himself to a CEO. God reveals himself in the pages of his Holy Book, and faith is less a matter of smarts and more a matter of surrender.

"Speak, LORD, for your servant hears."[3]

God wants to be known—and he calls his people to make him known. Christians don't keep God's revelation of himself through Christ as our pet secret. No, just as the nation of Israel was sent into the world to be a blessing to the nations, so the church of Jesus Christ is sent into the world to carry this message of *life*: God can be *known* through his Son Jesus.[4] All four of the Gospels end with a commissioning of the church for the mission of God.

God's people are sent as Jesus himself was sent. In fact, the miraculous catch of fish recorded here calls to mind an earlier story and promise of Jesus as recorded in Luke 5. When Jesus called his disciples to follow him, he gave them a cosmic purpose: I will make you fishers of men. As Jesus restores Peter (three times for his thrice betrayal), the Great Shepherd is commissioning other shepherds to feed his sheep, even to lay down their lives. As we know from history, all eleven disciples were persecuted, martyred, or exiled for their faith.

The story of the Bible is a story of grace from first to last. It is the story of God's speaking and God's serving. God calls—and wills himself to be known. God cleanses—and circumcises the hearts of his bent and crooked people. God communes—and makes it possible for us to enjoy his friendship. God commissions—and sends his church into the world bearing emphatically good news.

Christ has died. Christ has risen. Christ will come again.

How will you respond?

For Reflection/Discussion

How much hope does Peter's story of betrayal then restoration give to you? If you believe the message of Jesus, what habits of mission might you take up to tell others this good news?

DARIUS RACKUS

"God had picked me up, taken me from being his opponent, and put me on his side."

Darius Rackus grew up in a family with nominal Christian faith. "We were Christmas and Easter Catholics." His mother, raised in Eastern Europe, valued Catholicism as an expression of cultural and national pride. Before his family moved from Canada to the United States when he was twelve, Darius attended Catholic school, although less for the religious formation and more for the academic rigor. "There was no belief in God, no prayer, no Scripture in our house. We were your traditional North American secular family."

Late in high school, Darius decided to study science in university. "Because science had disproven God, I donned the costume of an atheist." He was anomalous in his group of friends, the majority of whom were at least occasional churchgoers. "I thought atheism was required for studying science." But as Darius began his undergraduate education at Durham University in the United Kingdom, his atheistic assumptions were quickly challenged in his science courses. "In chemistry, we were learning quantum mechanics and atomic structure and how these equations explain such complexity and such simplicity at the same time. In biology, we were studying ecosystems and environments, all these complicated interconnected systems that seemed to be stable and to have these codependencies. Both of those things—the smallest of the smallest things and the largest systems in our earth—really didn't scream to me, 'There is no God.'" Confronted with the beauty, the simplicity, and the complexity of the material universe, Darius became "open" to theism—and the idea of God.

His spiritual search began more in earnest when late one night, having exhausted all the BBC comedy programs he usually listened to online in order to fall asleep, he tuned into the program "Humphrys in Search of God." The host, John Humphrys, had been raised in an Anglican church but, when confronted with the weight of the world's collective suffering, had abandoned his childhood faith. In this four-part series, Humphrys returned to religious questions, which he put to a variety of faith leaders (rabbis, imams, pastors, and priests).

An interview with an Anglican bishop particularly piqued Darius's interest and prompted him to reconsider some of his misconceptions of God. "The bishop was saying that a lot of people have the idea of God as this man with a big flowing beard, sitting up in the clouds, handing things down on stone tablets to other men with equally long flowing beards." The bishop argued that this belittled the idea of God. He went on to talk about the evidence for God in the created world—like "the bonds between atoms and a lot of stuff that was making sense of what I was learning as an undergraduate," Darius remembered. "That got me thinking, *Maybe there is a God.*" Armed with his important (and new-to-him) discovery, several weeks later he announced to a friend whom he knew to be a Christian: "David, I think there might be a God."

His friend began inviting him to Bible studies and group meetings sponsored by a student fellowship called Christian Union. At his first Bible study, hosted in a dorm room, Darius felt completely disoriented in the unfamiliar setting. "Everyone had their Bibles out, and the translations were different. I was trying to follow along, but my words didn't match what was being read. They were talking about Moses being a shadow of Jesus, and it was all really weird and awkward." Previously, Darius had dismissed the relevance of the Bible: "It was very easy to pick a conspiracy theory to discredit the Bible. My thought was that there are dozens of these theories, and because they exist, Scripture surely doesn't need to be addressed."

At his first large group meeting hosted by Durham's Christian Union, students gathered to share the Christian albums and books that had most recently inspired them—clearly topics of insider baseball for someone standing on the outside. "Someone saw me and must have thought, 'What's he doing here?'" Wisely, this person grabbed a copy of *Christianity Explored*, a short book that explored the meaning of the life, death, and resurrection of Jesus through the Gospel of Mark. "I haven't read this one in a while," this person said, "but we have a lot of copies here, and it's one I would definitely recommend." After the meeting ended, Darius took a copy home and began reading. If he nurtured remaining suspicions about the reliability of the Bible, he found that *Christianity Explored* quickly waylaid them. "One of the things [the book] does is that it starts off by saying, look, you may have doubts about Scripture. We're just going to take this one piece of it, the Gospel of Mark. [This book] claims to be an eyewitness account of events that happened, which would make it a historical document. Let's give it the benefit of the doubt and see what it is trying to communicate, what it's trying to say." At the same time, another friend from Christian Union began offering to read the Bible one-on-one with Darius. They'd meet weekly, exploring small New Testament passages and discussing them together. Although he knew he could read and learn a lot from the Bible on his own, Darius also understood that reading with someone else helped to illuminate it even more.

"There was never this get-on-your-knees-and-pray moment," Darius reflected as he traced the arc of his conversion to Christian faith, "never one day when it all clicked." But if there was any kind of epiphany, it happened while reading Romans 5 with his friend. Darius had been struck in particular with verses 8–10: "But God shows his love for us in that while we were still sinners, Christ died for us. Since, therefore, we have now been justified by his blood, much more shall we be saved by him from the wrath of God. For if while we were enemies we were reconciled to God by the death of his Son, much more, now that we are reconciled, shall we be saved by his life."

"When we were reading that," Darius explained, "I had this image in my mind of a big battle scene in *Braveheart*. The English army was lined up on one side—and the quivering Scots on the other side. Whatever your view of history, I was on the wrong side. That's when I realized: it's not just about assenting to some historical ideas or holding to some facts that you should believe. Christian faith and life are really a response to something that God has already done. God had picked me up, taken me from being his opponent, and put me on his side."

Darius Rackus has been following Jesus for thirteen years and is now a husband, father, and full-time researcher in chemistry.

EPILOGUE

On September 11, 2001, the world was violently severed into before and after. More recently, there has been another violent cleaving. We have not watched planes fly into the Manhattan skyline, but we have watched the world shutter when the WHO declared a global pandemic on March 11, 2020. These kinds of events invoke our vulnerability. We lead a terribly fragile existence and, despite our technological advances, enjoy far less control than we think.

Our family returned to Canada from our spring vacation just before borders closed, airlines curtailed service, and death was plotted daily on a curve. For the first several weeks, we watched the world primarily through our front window. Early one morning, when the pandemic was our new and disorienting reality, paramedics came for my elderly neighbor across the street. They donned masks and helped each other tie their long blue gowns closed.

We waited to see who they would wheel out on their stretcher.

I feared less for Sue, whom I wrote about in Day 2. In her mid-eighties, she still shovels her own driveway and tends a sprawling garden. Her husband, on the other hand, has been stooped by the years, and it had been a near miracle when he made a brief appearance last spring at a neighborhood gathering. On the occasions that Richard does emerge from the house, shuffling behind his walker, it's usually to read to crowded classrooms of schoolchildren in one of Toronto's most diverse—and poor—neighborhoods.

We kept our vigil, and half an hour later, Richard was strapped to a gurney, drinking in oxygen, and on his way to a local hospital. Weeks later, to everyone's relief and surprise, he returned.

When the curtain of pandemic fell, in a matter of days, the world became almost instantly unrecognizable. A trip to the grocery store became a rare excursion. Church went virtual. Schools were closed, and working parents assumed homeschooling responsibilities. As a bit of good news, people who had given scant thought to God suddenly found themselves praying.

After New York City emerged as an early epicenter of the virus, Dr. Sylvie de Souza, chair of emergency medicine at Brooklyn Hospital Center, was interviewed by the *New York Times.* Supplies had been running precariously short, and de Souza worried that the emergency room would be out of space in a week.

The fear was palpable in the article, which was published in late March. So too was the faith. As another tenuous morning dawned, "the health workers in the tent lifted their arms at a safe distance, as if they were holding hands, and said a prayer—to make the right decisions; to be protected, along with their patients, from the disease." Dr. de Souza told the *Times* reporter that she planned to make this a kind of ritual for her staff. "That's all we can do: just pray, stick together, encourage each other, not get paralyzed by fear."[1]

Only weeks previous, a staff prayer at a publicly funded hospital would have been unimaginable. In a pandemic, however, faith became a thing to cling to, without embarrassment or apology. Some might call it an evolutionary reflex in the face of fear. But I'm not nearly so cynical. I can't help but wonder if we aren't instead reaching out toward the real, hoping to grasp something more powerful and more permanent than ourselves.

For the last forty days, I have tried to make sense of the habit of faith in the context of contemporary life. I've tried to surface questions as well as faithfully convey the answers the Bible offers. As I wrote in my introduction, I've hoped to give a very careful consideration of these sacred texts, Deuteronomy and John, as a help to those exploring Christian faith as well as to those already committed to it. But that's not all I've tried to do. Most of all, I've tried to illuminate how the story of the Bible is going somewhere purposeful: to the climactic moment when God entered human history as Jesus of Nazareth and shared our suffering, then rose from the dead to declare that death, the final enemy, was defeated. This is a story to make sense of our longings for a better world.

A couple of Christmases ago, my husband and I sat behind the orchestra for a performance of Handel's *Messiah*. Our discount tickets turned out to be the best seats in the house. When Canadian baritone Brett Polegato began singing the text of 1 Corinthians 15 (*Behold! I tell you a mystery. We shall not all sleep, but we shall all be changed*), I could see a small, gray-haired woman in the third row bring her hands to her face and begin to sob.

As Polegato sang this ancient Christian hope, the woman alternated between sobs and riveted gaze. She worked to compose herself, dabbing her eyes and her forehead with her handkerchief. Her daughters, flanking her sides, gave reassuring looks. But nearly half of the eight-minute aria, which the media described as spellbinding, she heard through tears. From my seat, I was captured less by Polegato and more by this patron. I wondered if she'd recently been wrecked by grief—or was just suddenly seized by the beauty of the gospel.

The trumpet will sound, and the dead will be raised.

As John the Evangelist wrote, faith is about coming to believe this story—and also the habit of continuing in it. In my own life of faith, daily Bible reading has been a keystone habit for continuing in belief—one small practice effecting incremental, if also monumental, change. I'm not as faithful as I'd like to be in studying or memorizing the Bible, and I find myself far more forgetful in middle age, struggling to recall references to familiar passages learned long ago. Still, most mornings, before the sun rises, I can be found sitting in an armchair in my living room, imbibing the words of Scripture.

I will say that there are days—and strings of days—when I seem to be impervious to God's words. They sit on my skin like glistening drops of water, and I feel myself disinterested, distracted by the errant jogger I glimpse from the front window. But there are other days, not altogether rare, when I hold audience with the Creator of the universe—or rather, when he holds audience with me. Stilled, I become "a tree planted by water, that sends out its roots by the stream, and does not fear when heat comes, for its leaves remain green, and is not anxious in the year of drought, for it does not cease to bear fruit."[2] I am learning to trust, however I feel on any given day, that this daily habit of faith is rooting me deep.

GROUP DISCUSSION GUIDE

Your group will optimally include both people who identify as Christians as well as people who are exploring the Christian faith. One obvious challenge in such a setting is learning to be genuinely hospitable to differing viewpoints. At Redeemer Presbyterian Church in New York City, groups like these are a regular feature of church life. Founding Pastor Tim Keller explains how they function at the opening of his book *Making Sense of God*: "Each person is . . . urged to be open to critique and willing to admit flaws and problems in their way of looking at things."[1] Humility, then, will be in order for these groups.

To structure a group discussion, leaders might decide to choose some of the questions at the end of the daily readings and combine them with some of the discussion questions below. (Attempting all of the questions will undoubtedly prove too zealous). As an additional note, questions 6–8 are the same for each week. I encourage groups to read aloud the selected passages as they begin their discussion.

Week 1: Introduction, Days 1–5 (Days 1, 5)

Read aloud Deuteronomy 1:1–8; 4:9–13.

1. If you're uncertain about or exploring the Christian faith, what do you find unfamiliar about faith in general or Christianity in particular?

2. Let's catch up on the story of Israel and Moses before the time of Deuteronomy. Collectively, what do we know?
3. What does the Hebrew title of Deuteronomy mean? How is this meaningful for understanding the life of faith?
4. What did we learn about the idea of *covenant* in this week's readings? What does *covenant* tell us about the God of the Bible?
5. On a scale of 1–10, how much confidence do you have that the Bible has relevant things to say today? Would you consider it authoritative?
6. From this week's readings, what confirmed your previously held assumptions? What challenged them?
7. What outstanding questions would you still like answered?
8. What practical insight about the life of faith was most illuminating for you personally? How will you apply it?

Week 2: Days 6–10 (Days 6, 9)

Read aloud Deuteronomy 5:6–21; 8:11–20.

1. Why is Mount Sinai such an important event for the nation of Israel?
2. How should we understand the "thou shalts" and "thou shalt nots" of the Ten Commandments? What's more hopeful about these rules than you might previously have imagined?
3. What's a working definition of *sin* as defined in Deuteronomy? How does that differ from what you previously thought?
4. What were some of the lessons Israel was meant to learn in the wilderness? How were they warned about prosperity?

5. As you learn more about the story of Israel, in what ways do you discover that you're like the Israelites?
6. From this week's readings, what confirmed your previously held assumptions? What challenged them?
7. What outstanding questions would you still like answered?
8. What practical insight about the life of faith was most illuminating? How will you apply it?

Week 3: Days 11–15 (Days 11, 15)

Read aloud Deuteronomy 10:1–11; 28:1–6, 15–19.

1. If it's true that "to be human is to long for home," how have you felt the acute longing for home in your own life?
2. The ancient sensibilities of Deuteronomy can make for difficult reading. Do you find yourself doubting the reliability of the Bible? Why or why not?
3. In Deuteronomy, obedience to God is understood as a means to human flourishing. How does this counter our cultural notions of freedom and autonomy?
4. What truths do the ceremonies of blessings and curses affirm? Should we assume that pain is always a punishment from God?
5. Is it selfish to want God's blessings? What does Deuteronomy say about the "self-interest" of faith?
6. From this week's readings, what confirmed your previously held assumptions? What challenged them?
7. What outstanding questions would you still like answered?
8. What practical insight about the life of faith was most illuminating? How will you apply it?

Week 4: Days 16–20 (Days 16, 20)

Read aloud Deuteronomy 29:1–9; 33:26–29.

1. What are some of the "signs and wonders" God performed on Israel's behalf?
2. According to Deuteronomy, are signs and wonders sufficient for faith? Why or why not?
3. What is Israel's spiritual problem according to Deuteronomy? What's the proposed solution?
4. If it's true that the Bible is "God-centric" as we learned early in our readings, what have we learned so far about the nature of God?
5. Did you expect Deuteronomy to end as it did? What conclusions can we draw that despite the gloomy forecast for Israel's future, Deuteronomy ends on a note of blessing?
6. From this week's readings, what confirmed your previously held assumptions? What challenged them?
7. What outstanding questions would you still like answered?
8. What practical insight about the life of faith was most illuminating? How will you apply it?

Week 5: Days 21–25 (Days 21, 23)

Read aloud John 1:14–18; 3:16–21.

1. How much familiarity do you have with the four Gospels: Matthew, Mark, Luke, and John? What surprised you about these first chapters of the Gospel of John?
2. On a scale of 1–10, how reliable do you think these Gospels are as historical accounts of Jesus's life?
3. What connections can we make between Deuteronomy and John, even between Moses and Jesus, from this week's

readings? Is there anything that was "dim" in Deuteronomy that now seems to be illumined?

4. Jesus told his first curious disciples to "come and see." What do you personally find compelling about the invitation? What would make you hesitate?
5. What evidence do we find in this week's reading for the *exclusive* claims of Jesus as well as his radically *inclusive* love?
6. From this week's readings, what confirmed your previously held assumptions? What challenged them?
7. What outstanding questions would you still like answered?
8. What practical insight about the life of faith was most illuminating? How will you apply it?

Week 6: Days 26–30 (Days 26, 30)

Read aloud John 6:60–71; 11:38–44.

1. What are the seven important "signs" that Jesus performed—and John recorded—in this Gospel? What is the purpose of these signs?
2. In the crowds around Jesus, we find the curious, the doubting, the believing, and even the angry. To whom do you relate the most?
3. For what do human beings "hunger" and "thirst" in their lives? What would it mean for you personally to trust that Jesus alone will satisfy your deepest desires?
4. How does this Gospel seem to insist that following Jesus entails more than cerebral assent to certain ideas about Jesus?
5. Does Jesus's promise of resurrection and eternal life feel like a pie-in-the-sky hope—or something to be trusted as true? Explain.

6. From this week's readings, what confirmed your previously held assumptions? What challenged them?
7. What outstanding questions would you still like answered?
8. What practical insight about the life of faith was most illuminating? How will you apply it?

Week 7: Days 31–35 (Days 31, 34)

Read aloud John 12:27–36; 15:1–11.

1. What evidence did John offer to his readers to illustrate that Jesus is both fully God and fully human? If we didn't uphold his divinity and his humanity, what would happen to our understanding of Jesus?
2. John presented Jesus as a king bearing a cross. What does the surprise of a cross-bearing king reveal to us about the life of faith?
3. What insights from John allow us to see that Jesus is the "solution" to humanity's moral crookedness—a condition we saw illumined in Deuteronomy?
4. Many assume that faith has to do with the self-effort of strenuous religious practice. What did we learn from this week's readings that rejects that assumption?
5. The cross is central to John's narrative. What clues about the cross did John scatter through his Gospel, long before we got to the actual event? What do we learn about its meaning?
6. From this week's readings, what confirmed your previously held assumptions? What challenged them?
7. What outstanding questions would you still like answered?
8. What practical insight about the life of faith was most illuminating? How will you apply it?

Week 8: Days 36–40, Epilogue (Days 38, 39)

Read aloud John 19:17–30; 20:11–18.

1. What surprises you about the details that are included and omitted from the scene at Golgotha? What might be John's purpose in shaping his account in this way?
2. What details make for compelling evidence that the story of Jesus's resurrection is a historical account? Do you find them convincing?
3. How do the first disciples to encounter the living Christ respond: Mary, Peter, John, Thomas?
4. Considering Jesus's interaction with Thomas, how should we relate to our own doubts and desires for proof?
5. If the resurrection is true, what does it change? If it isn't true, what would be left of the Christian faith?
6. From this week's readings, what confirmed your previously held assumptions? What challenged them?
7. What outstanding questions would you still like answered?
8. What practical insight about the life of faith was most illuminating? How will you apply it?

NOTES

Acknowledgments

1. Margaret Atwood, *Negotiating with the Dead* (Cambridge, UK: Anchor, 2002), xix.

Introduction

1. *Educated*, a memoir by Tara Westover, describes just such a childhood in a fundamentalist Mormon home.
2. This is a way of referring to those who self-identify as atheist or agnostic.
3. I highly recommend Joshua Chatraw's *Telling a Better Story.*
4. Scientist and philosopher Michael Polanyi writes about the "preunderstanding" that forms our knowing in his work *Personal Knowledge.*
5. Diogenes Allen, *Three Outsiders: Pascal, Kierkegaard, Simone Weil* (Eugene, OR: Wipf and Stock, 1983), 39–40.
6. In speaking with Lauren McAfee, coauthor of *Not What You Think: Why the Bible Might Be Nothing We Expected Yet Everything We Need* (Grand Rapids: Zondervan, 2019), she offhandedly mentioned research by YouVersion, a Bible reading app. They've discovered that people who spend the most time on the app are those keeping track of their Bible reading "streak." We're incented to beat our own records.
7. Matthew 11:28–30.

A Note to the Reader

1. Learn more from *Atomic Habits* by James Clear.

Mark Lawrence

1. The line is actually, "Therefore that he may raise, the Lord throws down." John Donne, "Hymn to God, My God, in My Sickness," Poetry Foundation,

accessed September 1, 2020, https://www.poetryfoundation.org/poems/44114/hymn-to-god-my-god-in-my-sickness.

Day 1 Lend Me Your Ears

1. The Old Testament was originally written in Hebrew, although one important translation called the Septuagint was written in Greek.
2. Genesis 1:1; 12:1–3.
3. Exodus 19–20.
4. Exodus 34:6–7.
5. William Shakespeare, *Julius Caesar*, act 3, scene 2.

Day 2 Oh, the Places You'll Go

1. As Peter Leithart explains in *A House for My Name*, when Adam and Eve were exiled from the garden of Eden because of their sin, they traveled east. For this reason, "east" has an ominous connotation in the biblical story.
2. In her book, *Bearing God's Name*, Carmen Joy Imes points out the interesting literary structure of the Sinai narratives. Before Sinai and after Sinai (which is to say, between Exodus 19 and Numbers 10), there seem to be deliberate parallelisms, which would suggest Mount Sinai as the high point in the narrative.

Day 3 Mirror, Mirror, on the Wall

1. Genesis 1:1, emphasis added.
2. In Genesis 12:3, God promises Abraham that in him "all the families of the earth shall be blessed."
3. Numbers 22–24.
4. Genesis 25:19–27:46.
5. Genesis 13; 14; 19.
6. Some scholars say this language of total destruction was ancient euphemism, meaning simply that victory was secured. See Gordon K. Oeste and William J. Webb, *Bloody, Brutal and Barbaric? Wrestling with Troubling War Texts* (Downers Grove, IL: InterVarsity Press, 2019).

Day 4 No Do-Over

1. When the Israelites first arrived at Kadesh Barnea, they sent twelve spies on a scouting mission. Ten returned to say that it would be utterly impossible for them to take the land; two trusted God's promise to give it to them (cf. Num. 14:6–9).
2. The Pentateuch is another name for the first five books of the Bible.
3. Read Exodus 3 and 4 to hear Moses list the reasons why he is the wrong person for the job when God calls him to lead Israel out of Egypt. "Oh, my Lord, please send someone else" (Exod. 4:13).
4. This is an insight gleaned from Tim Keller's wonderful book, *Prayer* (New York: Penguin, 2016).
5. See Luke 11:13.

Day 5 To Have and to Hold

1. See Deuteronomy 4:23.

2. To be most technical, an ancient covenant was "cut" between two parties, referring to the rite of cutting an animal to ratify an agreement. I. Howard Marshall, A. R. Millard, J. I. Packer, and D. J. Wiseman, eds., *New Bible Dictionary*, 3rd ed. (Downers Grove, IL: InterVarsity Press, 1996), 234.

3. It was our Gospel writer John who said this in one of his letters (1 John 4:19).

4. Bruce C. Birch, *Let Justice Roll Down* (Louisville: Westminster, 1991), 153.

Day 6 The Moment Called Now

1. I'm thankful for this insight from Carmen Imes in her book, *Bearing God's Name*. She credits it to her professor, Daniel Block.

2. See N. T. Wright, *After You Believe: Why Christian Character Matters.*

3. William J. U. Philip, "The Law of Promise," *PT Media Papers* 3 (2003): 12.

Day 7 Practice Your Lines

1. This can sound like the corrupt stealing of land from indigenous people that has blighted the history in North America. However, in Genesis 15:16, God tells Abraham that he is not giving him the land of Canaan for another 400 years because "the iniquity of the Amorites is not yet complete." God did judge the Canaanites' sin, and for this reason, they lost their land.

2. The words from Numbers 15:37–41 were also included.

3. Maimonides, Hilkhot Tefillin u-Mezuzah 6:13, quoted in Jeffrey H. Tigay, *The JPS Torah Commentary: Deuteronomy* (Philadelphia: The Jewish Publication Society, 1996), 444.

Day 8 His Name Is Jealous

1. Exodus 34:14.

2. One scholar has suggested that "betrothed" is a closer translation to the Hebrew word most often translated as "holy" in Deuteronomy 7:6.

3. Richard Dawkins, *The God Delusion* (Boston: Houghton Mifflin, 2006), 31.

4. It was always an option for the Canaanite people to join Israel as Rahab did (see Josh. 2).

Day 9 Fieldnotes from the Wilderness

1. Luke 18:22.

Day 10 Signs and Wonders

1. Exodus 20:20.

2. Exodus 3:1–6.

3. Lauren Winner, *Wearing God* (New York: HarperOne, 2015), 206.

4. Numbers 11:1–3.

5. Exodus 17:1–7.

6. Numbers 11:4–35.

7. Robert Robinson, "Come Thou Fount of Every Blessing," 1758, public domain.

Day 11 There's No Place Like Home

1. Genesis 1:1.

2. I am paraphrasing what I learned from Carmen Joy Imes in *Bearing God's Name* (Downers Grove, IL: InterVarsity Press, 2019), 41.

Day 12 Five Words of Faith

1. Tigay, *The JPS Torah Commentary: Deuteronomy*, 110.

Day 13 Worrying for God's Reputation

1. Some would point to Deuteronomy 17:14–20 as evidence that Israel functioned more like a theocratic constitutional monarchy. God would elect the king, who would write for himself a copy of the Torah. God's teaching would effectively function like a constitution.

2. Deuteronomy 22:1.

3. This was suggested to me in the interview I did with Carmen Joy Imes for *Christianity Today*, which appeared in the December 2019 issue.

4. This is from a talk titled "Is God a Misogynist?" that Mary Willson gave at the 2016 TGCW Conference, https://www.thegospelcoalition.org/conference_media/is-god-a-misogynist/.

Day 14 The Question of Appetite

1. This may seem an impossible task, but a partial copy of the Code of Hammurabi, a Babylonian law code, is on display at the Louvre museum in Paris. Its 282 laws are inscribed on a 7.5-foot tall stone stele. Two of these steles would have easily accommodated Deuteronomy's law code.

2. See Judges 19–21.

3. John 6:67.

Day 15 No Mercenary Affair

1. What struck me in this particular list of curses was that parents were cursed to eat their own children. There is something deeply degrading about the nature of sin.

2. C. S. Lewis, *The Weight of Glory* (New York: HarperOne, 1980), 26.

Day 16 No Cherry-Cheeked Santa Claus

1. Allen, *Three Outsiders*, 28.

2. Tigay, *The JPS Torah Commentary: Deuteronomy*, 279–80.

3. Genesis 19.

4. Lot's wife was initially convinced of the coming judgment on Sodom, although as the family fled, she disobeyed the command not to look back. She was turned into a pillar of salt (Gen. 19:26).

5. Genesis 19:14.

6. In the garden of Eden, God said that his people would die for their sin. After they ate the fruit, however, they continued to live, even if in exile. Physical death came much later, and God's immediate curses fell on the ground as well as the work that it would take to cultivate its "thorns and thistles" (Gen. 3:17–19).

Day 17 Heart Surgery

1. Deuteronomy 4:1.

2. Deuteronomy 6:24.

3. See Luke 15:11–32.

Day 18 The With-God Life

1. At the age of forty, Moses had to escape from Egypt after he murdered an Egyptian in defense of an Israelite. He spent the next forty years shepherding his father-in-law's herds in the wilderness.

2. Exodus 33:7–11.

3. Exodus 34:29–35.

Day 19 The Laboring God

1. Isaiah 42:14.

2. Robert Alter, *The Five Books of Moses* (New York: W.W. Norton & Company, 2004), 1039.

3. Some might feel uncomfortable with my phrasing here, but Hosea 11 gives us this picture of a God bent on punishing his people for their sin, then recoiling from his own anger. "How can I give you up?" he asks, feeling his own compassion warm within him.

4. "Faithful are the wounds of a friend; profuse are the kisses of an enemy" (Prov. 27:6).

Day 20 The Bookends of Blessing

1. Nina Riggs, *The Bright Hour* (New York: Simon and Schuster, 2017), 207.

2. Julie Yip-Williams, *The Unwinding of the Miracle* (New York: Random House, 2019), 7.

3. Psalm 90:12.

4. Psalm 90:10.

5. Genesis 13:15.

6. In the New Testament, the writer of Hebrews tells us that "faith is the assurance of things hoped for, the conviction of things not seen" (Heb. 11:1).

7. Genesis 49:26.

8. Genesis 1:28.

9. Romans 7:15, 24.

Day 21 Where We Left Off

1. John 20:31.

2. Frederick Dale Bruner, *The Gospel of John: A Commentary* (Grand Rapids: Eerdmans, 2012), 32.

3. It's important to note that unlike other world religions founded prior to the printing press, Christianity is the only one that has written biographical accounts of its founder's life that circulated within living memory of his death.

4. Robert W. Funk, "Jesus Seminar Opening Remarks," Westar Institute, March 1985, https://www.westarinstitute.org/projects/jesus-seminar-opening-remarks/.

Day 22 That Wine Will Preach

1. 1 Corinthians 15:32.

2. Jeremiah 31:12; Deuteronomy 7:13.

3. See Genesis 49:11.

4. Many call John 1–12 the "Book of Signs."

5. Paul's letters were written before the Gospel of John. They are some of our earliest historical records about Jesus.

6. 1 Corinthians 1:22–24.

Day 23 On Getting Fidgety

1. Bruner, *The Gospel of John*, 166.

2. 2 Corinthians 5:17.

3. Lesslie Newbigin, *The Light Has Come* (Grand Rapids: Eerdmans, 1982), 37.

4. Ezekiel 36:25–27.

5. Rebecca McLaughlin, *Confronting Christianity* (Wheaton: Crossway, 2019), 48–49.

6. Newbigin, *The Light Has Come*, 43.

Day 24 A Ringing World of Praise

1. Robert Alter, *The Art of Biblical Narrative* (New York: Basic Books, 2011), 60.

2. Examples of this type-scene are Genesis 24:10–61 and Exodus 2:16–21.

3. Jewish and Samaritan people did not associate. In fact, this is the reason for the woman's chagrin when Jesus asks her for a drink. She knows that he, a Jew, should disdain drinking from any vessel shared by a Samaritan.

4. McLaughlin, *Confronting Christianity*, 38, 42.

5. C. S. Lewis, *Reflections on the Psalms* in *The Complete C. S. Lewis Signature Classics* (New York: HarperCollins, 2002), 178–79.

6. 1 Corinthians 10:4.

Day 25 The Great Mystery

1. When Jesus told the lame man in verse 8 to take up his bed, the Pharisees accused him of commanding the man to violate the strict Sabbath prohibition against carrying a load. See Jeremiah 17:21–22.

2. Robert Farrar Capon, *Kingdom, Grace, Judgment* (Grand Rapids: Eerdmans, 2002), 19.

3. John allusively refers to Jesus's baptism in verse 37. Matthew and Luke fill in the details about what God said that day by the Jordan River: "This is my beloved Son, with whom I am well pleased" (Matt. 3:17).

Day 26 God's Gift of Bread

1. We know that only the men were numbered, so with the additional women and children, this crowd might have filled a decent-sized basketball arena.

2. See Exodus 3.

3. Jesus's answer can also be translated, "It is I." In the Greek, *eimi*, which includes both subject and verb, means "I am." The use of *ego* is emphatic. This indicates that Jesus is using an unusual and significant construction, which is the Greek equivalent of Yahweh.

Day 27 Identity Verification

1. Micah 5:2.

2. Luke 2:1–7.

3. It is also called the Feast of Tabernacles.

4. Isaiah 12:3.

5. Ezekiel 47.

6. C. S. Lewis, *Mere Christianity* in *The Complete C. S. Lewis Signature Classics* (New York: HarperCollins, 2002), 50–51.

Day 28 The Dawning of Day

1. See Day 15.

2. Michelle Van Loon, *Moments and Days* (Carol Stream, IL: NavPress/Tyndale, 2016), 82.

3. Gary Burge, *John* in the NIV Application Commentary Series (Grand Rapids: Zondervan, 2000), 279.

4. These "examinations," called "tests" or "scrutinies," were used by the early church to verify the truth of a person's intended commitment to Christ. First, they wanted to make sure no one had infiltrated the ranks of the church for nefarious purposes. Second, they wanted to make sure that people who announced a desire to follow Jesus really understood the implications of the decision.

5. Newbigin, *The Light Has Come*, 119.

Day 29 Born to Be Free

1. Psalm 23.

2. Numbers 27:16–17.

3. Psalm 78:71.

4. Isaiah 53:4–6.

5. It's an important note of context that Jesus is addressing his audience during the winter celebration of Hanukkah, or the Feast of the Dedication. This

holiday remembered a tragic failure in Jewish temple leadership during the reign of Antiochus Epiphanes IV of Syria. At that time, there were corrupt, sell-out priests, and the result was a time of tragic persecution for the Jewish people. Antiochus decreed that sacred Jewish writings should be destroyed, that the practice of Jewish faith should be prohibited, and that the Jewish temple should become a sanctuary for Zeus. His singular, blasphemous act was sacrificing a pig on the temple altar. But he was met with courageous revolt. Judas Maccabeus fought against Greek oppressors, secured victory for the Jewish people, and reconsecrated the temple for worship. The memory of "thieves and robbers" and "hired hands" was all too vivid in that Maccabean history.

Day 30 Dead Man Walking

1. According to Jewish tradition, the soul lingered for three days, hoping to reenter the body.
2. Exodus 33:19.
3. This Scripture, taken from Isaiah 61:1–2, provides the text for Jesus's first sermon as recorded in Luke 4:16–20.
4. Deuteronomy 28:1–14.
5. Bruner, *The Gospel of John*, 663.
6. Luke 23:46.

Day 31 Hail to the Chief

1. Historically, this waving of palm branches had been the way that the Jews hailed their national heroes in the middle of the second century BC, including Simon Maccabeus (after he conquered Jerusalem) and Judas Maccabeus (after he reconsecrated the temple).
2. Psalm 118:27; John 1:29, 36.
3. Numbers 21:4–9.
4. 1 Corinthians 1:23.
5. Deuteronomy 29:2–4.
6. Hebrews 12:1–2.
7. Deuteronomy 8:3.

Day 32 Undercover Boss

1. See Andy Crouch's, *Playing God: Redeeming the Gift of Power*.
2. In the Greek, the same term for "to lay down" is used in both John 13:4 and John 10:18.
3. Burge, *John*, 383.
4. Titus 3:4–6.
5. John 12:31; see Bruner, *The Gospel of John*, 755.

Day 33 Last Will and Testament

1. Luke 24:13–35.
2. Andy Crouch opens his book *Playing God* with a wonderful reflection on the grammar God used in the garden when he said, "Let there be": "By saying

'Let there be,' the Creator God makes room for more being, for more agents who could utter their own 'let it be,'" Andy Crouch, *Playing God* (Westmont, IL: InterVarsity Press, 2013), 32.

3. This idea—of following the vertical and horizontal beams of the cross—was originally Lesslie Newbigin's.

Day 34 The Hard Work of Staying Put

1. In case you're curious, several lines later, the poem turns in a happier direction:

> Together, despite winters, we have resurrected
> twenty springs
> and what can be lovelier than all that is
> perennial?

2. Hosea 10:1; Psalm 80:8–11; Ezekiel 19:10; Isaiah 5:1–7; 11:1. Also, to testify to the ubiquity of this image, coins minted during the brief Jewish revolt against Rome (AD 68–70) were stamped with the image of a vine. See Newbigin, *The Light Has Come*, 196.

3. See Day 11.

4. Exodus 33:11.

5. 1 Corinthians 3:16; 2 Corinthians 6:16; Ephesians 2:21.

6. See Matthew 11:28–30.

7. Alan Kreider, *The Patient Ferment of the Early Church* (Grand Rapids: Baker Academic, 2016), 62.

Day 35 The Helper

1. Importantly, John the apostle, the writer of this Gospel, does not flee. He is at Jesus's side until Jesus takes his last heaving breath.

2. Newbigin, *The Light Has Come*, 210.

3. See 2 Peter 3:15–16.

4. Hebrews 4:12.

5. Burge, *John*, 215.

6. As we get to the resurrection account in a few chapters, we'll see how often it's repeated, "I have *seen* the Lord!"

7. 1 John 1:1–2.

8. Jesus's betrayer, Judas, committed suicide. See Matthew 27:3–5.

Day 36 The Lord's Prayer

1. Matthew 6:9–13.

2. Let's not forget Moses's prayer in Deuteronomy 3 (Day 4).

3. Matthew 26:36–56; Luke 22:39–46.

4. John 12:27–28.

5. McLaughlin, *Confronting Christianity*, 63.

Day 37 The Gospel Garden

1. John 20:31.

2. Psalms 2, 45, 89, 110. It was also a title used to speak of the coming Messiah in the four-hundred-year period between the two testaments.

3. This is the title of his popular book *How God Became King* (New York: HarperOne, 2012).

4. Burge, *John*, 515.

5. 2 Corinthians 12:9.

Day 38 The Finish Line

1. Gary Burge makes special note in his commentary that the Greek word used in verse 30 means not to give up his life as in to forfeit it, but to give up his life as in to hand it over. Burge, *John*, 529–30.

2. Philip J. Rhinelander, *The Faith of the Cross*, Paddock Lectures, General Theological Seminary, 1914 (New York: Longmans, Green and Co., 1916).

3. Exodus 12.

4. Exodus 12:13.

5. John 1:29.

6. He is buried in a wealthy man's tomb and embalmed with an exorbitant amount of spices.

Day 39 Closing Arguments

1. Lee Strobel, *The Case for Christ* (Grand Rapids: Zondervan, 2016), 51, 324.

2. 2 Corinthians 5:5.

3. 1 Peter 1:10–12.

Day 40 Revelation

1. Bruner, *The Gospel of John*, 1205.

2. Bruner, *The Gospel of John*, 1206.

3. 1 Samuel 3:9.

4. John 17:3.

Epilogue

1. Sheri Fink, "'We're in Disaster Mode,' Courage inside a Brooklyn Hospital Confronting Coronavirus," *New York Times*, updated April 15, 2020, https://www.nytimes.com/2020/03/26/nyregion/coronavirus-brooklyn-hospital.html.

2. Jeremiah 17:8.

Group Discussion Guide

1. Tim Keller, *Making Sense of God* (New York: Penguin, 2018), preface, Kindle.

Jen Pollock Michel is the award-winning author of *Teach Us to Want*, *Keeping Place*, and *Surprised by Paradox*. She holds a BA in French from Wheaton College and an MA in literature from Northwestern University. An American living in Toronto, Jen is a wife and mother of five. She is the lead editor for *Imprint* magazine, published by Grace Centre for the Arts, and host of the *Englewood Review of Books* podcast.

Connect with Jen

Head to **jenpollockmichel.com** to sign up for her monthly newsletter, to learn about her speaking, or to send her a message.

And follow her on social media!

jenpmichel

www.ingramcontent.com/pod-product-compliance
Lightning Source LLC
Chambersburg PA
CBHW030504100426
42813CB00002B/327
* 9 7 8 1 5 4 0 9 0 1 4 7 7 *